HUSTLE
AWAY DEBT

Eliminate Your Debt by Making More Money

DAVID CARLSON

founder of  Young Adult Money

D0963490

Forbes calls David Carlson's **Young Adult Money** one of the best personal finance websites.

ISBN 978-1-63353-335-6

DEDICATION

This book is dedicated to my wonderful wife who never fails to support and encourage me.

TABLE OF CONTENTS

I've been side hustling since my first lemonade stand. Personal assistant, virtual assistant, receptionist, tradeshow hostess, coat check girl, flyer distributor, drama instructor, babysitter, research subject – I've done it all. In fact, I've never been what you might consider "traditionally employed".

These days, however, my side hustle is no longer characterized by $10 to $20 an hour odd jobs serving as a financial lifeline. I've since scaled my hustle from a survival mechanism to a nearly six figure, and growing, business.

Let me assure you though, that this narrative of success is only my experience – it's not a promise.

I can't guarantee that you'll be successful in your side hustle.

I can't promise that you'll stumble upon a career you love.

I can't ensure that your hustle will generate earnings in excess.

But it can. It has for me and the many hustlers who came before and inspired my side hustle journey – here's why...

Side hustling is opportunity – a chance to be intentional, diversify and harness control over your income potential; a chance to kick start your debt pay off, amp up your retirement savings and reach your financial goals; a chance to build a life on your own terms!

For me, the side hustle was a chance to break free of the cycle of boom and bust I'd become accustomed to living as a professional actress in New York City. Initially motivated by survival, I side hustled to cover my bills until the next acting gig. It was limiting though.

Having grown tired of late nights closing at the restaurant followed by early morning auditions, I began to think bigger about my efforts. $10-20 an hour was a good way to make it to tomorrow, but it wasn't a way to build the life of my dreams.

I kept my restaurant, babysitting and personal assisting gigs to maintain cash flow, but simultaneously struck up another hustle, writing, with the intention of building something more sustainable and scalable.

My first foray into paid writing I got $20/article - not much of an improvement income-wise, so I challenged myself to ask for more. When clients wouldn't come to the negotiating table, I sought new clients that would. Slowly but surely, the requests got bigger - $30, $50, $100, $500, $2,000 - and soon, the paychecks were bigger too. So big in fact, that I found myself with more than a side hustle. I had a parallel career.

There was no singular miracle moment, no lightning strike that took my new side hustle and multiplied its value by 100, only the consistency of demanding more from myself, my work and my clients.

Side hustling is all about empowerment - using increased income potential to enable greater options and bring the life of your dreams within reach. To maximize that full potential though, you have to push yourself beyond the mindset of short-term survival and go for the big, outrageous fantasies that often exist only in your own imagination.

Making big requests brings these fantasies into fruition, if only in words. Eventually, if you keep asking aloud and delivering value in alignment with those requests, once seemingly unattainable aspirations can manifest in your reality.

I used to have this mantra, "six-figures by thirty" that I'd shout out to my boyfriend while heading out the door to pick up dry cleaning for someone I was assisting or taking the train out to Jersey for a kid I was babysitting. Today I'm 29 and against all odds, it's happening - my mantra is becoming my reality.

This book is filled with the mindset shifts and practical strategies you'll need to do the same. You'll learn the value of the side hustle, get concrete ideas on how you can develop your own, and start implementing the best practices to push you way past debt and launch you forward to financial freedom.

I know that in the moment, it might not seem glamorous or groundbreaking to go out and walk someone else's dog or clean someone else's house or change diapers on someone else's kid, but if you start the process and commit to your side hustle with the intensity and intention of creating something as big as your wildest dreams, you may find yourself stumbling upon a path that defies every limit you thought existed and opens doors to opportunities you never considered possible.

Happy hustling.

-Stefanie

INTRODUCTION

My wife and I got married soon after graduating from college. We were ready to start our lives together, both as newlyweds and as recent college graduates. We had dreams of buying a home, getting our masters degrees, and traveling. There was one thing that put a strain on both our relationship and finances: the nearly $100k we owed in student loans.

The $1,000+ payment we made each month on our student loans was a major drag on our finances. Even worse, these were minimum payments we were making; at this rate, we would have $1,000 going out the door every month for the next ten years.

Having so much money go towards student loans each month was, needless to say, debilitating. It's tough to pursue your dreams when you feel like you never have "enough" money.

Despite my job in corporate accounting, student loan debt on top of all the other expenses of daily life left a huge hole in our post-grad finances. While getting promotions at my day job had potential to help, promotions only happen so often. On a day-to-day basis, I had little to no ability to make more money at my 9-5.

My story is not uncommon. Over 70 percent of recent college graduates have student loans, and of those who have loans, the average 2015 college graduate had racked up a little more than $35,000 in debt[1]. The overall student loan debt level recently surpassed $1.2 trillion[2]. That's enough to not only put a strain on personal finances, but on an entire economy.

Even if a student graduates with no consumer or credit card debt, the impact of student loans can be crippling. Many millennials find themselves unable to pursue the dreams they had for their post-graduate lives.

As a personal finance blogger, I've read many posts focused on what people should do to avoid or minimize student loan debt. These posts may be helpful for high school students who are just starting college, but what about those who have already graduated and find themselves with a high amount of student loans?

One solution is cutting expenses. There are many advocates of this approach. In reality, though, expenses can only be cut so much. Cutting costs typically does not free up enough money to have a material impact on finances and also typically requires a downgrade in lifestyle.

Instead of focusing on cutting expenses and making difficult lifestyle changes, I strongly believe that focusing on making more money is the best approach for those who are in debt. The inevitable question people have in response to this is: "How exactly do I make more money?"

Instead of taking the traditional approach and focusing on making more at your 9–5, I have a better solution: side hustles.

When I use the phrase "side hustle" many people typically go, "Huh? What does that even mean?" Having a side hustle simply means having a source of income outside of your 9–5 that you work at in your free time. While you may not have control over how much you make at your 9–5, you have complete control over how much you make outside of your 9–5.

Over the past decade, I have had many side hustles. They range from working a weekend job to running my blog on nights and weekends. Despite the diversity of side hustles I've pursued, they all have one thing in common: they gave a noticeable boost to my finances.

To use a poker analogy, I have gone all in on side hustles since graduating college. I have done everything from freelance writing to a service I call "spreadsheet consulting." While every side hustle has required significant sacrifice, the benefit they have provided can't be overstated. The money I have been able to make in my free time has helped with student loans, car payments, and more.

While I currently have no intention of quitting my 9–5 and making a career out of one of my side hustles, I know many who have made this transition. It's just one of the many unexpected perks of having a side hustle.

From choosing the right side hustle for you, to giving you ideas for side hustles you can start, to exploring the unexpected (and awesome) benefits of having a side hustle, Hustle Away Debt will guide you through the process of starting a successful side hustle that will increase your income, help you pay off debt faster, and live a better life.

It's time to hustle away debt.

1. https://www.edvisors.com/newsletter/financial-aid-news-06-18-2015/

2. http://www.consumerfinance.gov/speeches/student-debt-swells-federal-loans-now-top-a-trillion/

Part

Side Hustle Primer

Understanding
Side Hustles

Chapter 1

I've worked in corporate finance for the past five-plus years. During this time, I worked extensively with Microsoft Excel and became pretty proficient with spreadsheets. After all, if you spend 4-8 hours a day 5 days a week on spreadsheets, you are bound to become pretty good at using them, especially if you are in an entry-level position looking for opportunities to stand out.

What does working on spreadsheets in an office cubicle have to do with side hustles, though?

A lot, actually.

A few years ago, a friend of mine who owns a small business emailed me saying he needed some help with his company's financial spreadsheets and my name was the first that came to mind. After discussing some of the problems and headaches the spreadsheets were causing him, we discussed what could be done to improve his files. He also mentioned that he had a budget for this project.

As a relatively new college graduate with a lot of student loans, I jumped at the opportunity to make some extra money outside of my full-time job. Making extra money wasn't the only advantage of this work though, as I was also improving skills that would be used at my full-time job. Other things I liked about the work was that it could be done remotely and whenever it fit into my schedule.

And that's how my "spreadsheet consulting" side hustle began.

Spreadsheet consulting is a good example of how side hustles can have unexpected benefits. More on that later on in the book.

I have not done any spreadsheet consulting for a couple of years, but I have been working at a couple of other side hustles. Later on in this chapter, I will share all of the side hustles I've done and how they've worked out for me.

Before I talk about my other side hustles, though, let's talk about side hustles in broader terms. After all, this book could very well be your first exposure to this concept.

Side hustles are ways to make money in addition to a 9-5 income. For example, when I worked on my friend's spreadsheets I was consulting for him on my evenings and weekends. It was by no means a replacement to my full-time income, but was certainly a way to supplement it.

A key concept to understand about side hustles is that they are extremely diverse. They can be as straightforward as a part-time job you fit in on evenings and weekends, or as complex as creating a product that you manufacture in China and sell online.

Side hustles may happen during set hours or they may be flexible from a time perspective. They may be location-independent (i.e. you can be sitting on your couch in your pajamas) or they may require you to be physically present. They may take just 3 hours of your free time or they may take 30. As long as the work fits within the definition of "making money in addition to a 9-5 income," it's a side hustle.

Understand your "Why"

People pursue side hustles for a wide variety of reasons. They include:

STUDENT LOANS

Millions upon millions of college graduates have student loan debt. I fall into this category, as my wife and I both graduated with a lot of student loan debt. My pursuit of side hustles – including starting YoungAdultMoney.com – was directly driven by our $1,000+ a month student loan payment. I didn't want my lifestyle and goals to suffer because of our student loans and was determined to offset the payments with extra income.

OTHER DEBT

Consumer debt, mortgages, and other debt can also drive people to look for additional income outside of their 9-5. A good example is someone with a car loan who is sick and tired of always having to take on new debt when they purchase a car. They can sit and complain about it or they can take action. One way they could be proactive is to utilize side hustles to pay off their car loan faster and start setting aside money to pay for their next car in cash.

SPECIFIC FINANCIAL GOALS

Having a specific financial goal to strive towards can motivate people to start a side hustle. Let's use an example that many people can relate to: travel. Let's say you want to travel but your current financial situation doesn't provide the income you need for the trips you desire to take. Making money in addition to your 9-5 could create a new income stream that can be used specifically for travel.

Another good example is home renovations. Let's say you are able to set aside $500 a month for home renovations. That means after a year you will have $6,000. Anyone who has a home knows that $6,000 doesn't go that far when it comes to home renovations. A retaining wall alone can cost $5,000 to $20,000, and that's just for a wall! If you can make an additional $1,000 a month through side hustles you can up the contributions to your home renovations account to $1,500 a month, which translates to $18,000 a year.

INCOME DIVERSIFICATION

Practically everyone has either been laid off from a job or knows at least one other person who has been laid off. With the boom-bust cycle our economy has experienced the past few decades combined with how quickly technology and startups disrupt entire business sectors, it's more important than ever to have a secondary income stream. No job – or industry – is safe.

I'm not suggesting that a side hustle will inevitably replace your full-time income (though it's an exciting idea for many), but having even some money coming in from a secondary income source can provide a safety net if you were to lose your primary income source. There are also many side hustles, like blogging, that typically pay no money the first 6-12 months. These side hustles are much easier to start when you have a full-time income than when you are in a situation where you need income ASAP.

ENTREPRENEURSHIP

There are many people out there who are entrepreneurial but, for one reason or another, are working a 9-5 job. I'm one of those people. Side hustles have allowed me to dabble in the small business sector without sacrificing my reliable and consistent 9-5 income.

Side hustles allow people to start a business without having to take on the full risk of relying solely on the business for income. If it succeeds, great! If it fails, there is usually only a small amount of money – if any – lost. While a side hustle entrepreneur may lose the time they devoted to a side hustle that fails, there is typically not the devastating financial loss that "full-time" entrepreneurs experience when their business fails.

When it comes to side hustles, it's absolutely essential to understand your "why." If you stick with side hustling long-term, there will be many situations where you get home from work after a long day at your 9-5 and don't want to do anything, let alone work more. This is one of the not-so-attractive aspects of side hustling and will require thinking back to your "why" to stay motivated.

As I already mentioned, my "why" is primarily student loan debt. I don't want my finances to be limited by the $1,000/month we put towards student loans. I want to be able to travel, buy a home, and do all the things I've dreamed of doing in my 20s and 30s.

I'm also driven by an entrepreneurial itch and desire for diversified income. In my ideal world, I would have my own business, or at minimum be in full control of both the work I do and my daily schedule. Don't get me wrong, there are many great jobs out there and there is nothing wrong with having a job, but most jobs typically do not fulfill an entrepreneurial drive. Thankfully, we live in a day and age where there are more opportunities to start and run a business in your free time than ever before.

Despite my interest in business, I have never been a full-time entrepreneur or business owner. I have had a job and been an employee since high school.

Being an employee has always been my primary income. Now that I have student loans it's almost unthinkable to quit my job to be a full-time business owner. Can you imagine the instability of not having a full-time paycheck? This is something most people with student loans or other debt have thought about. Perhaps some of you reading this are business owners already, but for myself and many others, the idea of quitting a full-time job for an entrepreneurial pursuit is a (financially) terrifying prospect.

Thankfully there are side hustles. Many side hustles have the potential to become a full-time job or business. For entrepreneurially-inclined people, that is a very attractive upside of certain side hustles.

As you read about my side hustles, you'll see the entrepreneurial side of me, but you'll also notice that not all of my side hustles are businesses. The purpose of sharing these is to both provide ideas for side hustles as well as give some real-life examples of how side hustles have impacted my life and how they could impact yours.

1) WORKING A PART-TIME JOB

Throughout college, I was a student worker in my University's IT department. It was a great job, but I wanted more. During my freshman year of college I took part in one of my first side hustles: a part-time job.

I worked on Friday nights and Saturdays at an office furniture moving company. When people moved cubicles, we'd move their boxes of stuff. We'd also move entire sections of cubicles and unload semi-trucks filled with equipment.

This was a great side hustle because it was flexible from a scheduling perspective. You could decide if you wanted to work or not each weekend as long as you told the scheduler by Wednesday. If you didn't want to or could not work, no problem. I also was able to work with one of my best friends. It's a little easier to sacrifice part of your weekend to make money when you are able to hang out with one of your best friends while doing it.

2) WORKING FOR A BLOG

Another way I've made side income was working for a blog. During my college days, I randomly met a personal finance blog owner through a political blog I had started. We ended up emailing and I eventually ended up doing blog work for him on a regular basis.

This was a great job for me as I got exposure to the operational aspect of blogs and gained valuable skills in business, marketing, and other things like search engine optimization. It gave me work experience that I could put on my resume and greatly benefited me when I finally started my own personal finance blog, Young Adult Money.

3) BLOGGING

I started blogging nearly ten years ago when I started a political blog. I eventually started writing for a group political blog as well. It was good experience but I made no money from it, so it wasn't a true side hustle. "Passion project" is a better description of my political blogging days.

In July of 2011, I started Young Adult Money. I didn't make a dime the first seven months despite the fact that I was posting 5-6 times a week, managing social media accounts, and doing all the important things you need to do to have a successful blog.

I finally started making money from blogging in 2012 and have made a small income from it ever since. I have been able to hire writers since then and have outsourced some of the work to free up time for things like writing this book. Blogging is by no means "easy" money, but there are many things about blogging that make it a very attractive side hustle. More on that later.

4) POKER

Some of you may be saying, "Wait, poker is just gambling! You cannot seriously be trying to convince me that poker is a side hustle!"

Hear me out.

Throughout college, I would regularly play poker both online and in person at card rooms. I never had a big payday like a couple others who I graduated from high school with (one pocketed over $300k from a single tournament and another won more than $200k in another tournament) but I did make a small amount of side income through playing.

While poker to some (or most) will result in losing money over time, when I was playing there were more players that had average to below-average skills. This allowed people who took the game seriously and gained above-average skills to make money over time.

5) SPREADSHEET CONSULTING

I shared earlier about my experience spreadsheet consulting, and I still think it was one of the best side hustles I've had. While it did require me to trade time for money, it allowed me to work on a skill that I use in my 9-5 while also allowing me to work from anywhere I wanted (at home, coffee shops, etc.).

One thing I learned from this side hustle is just how limited your time is when you side hustle. I would love to do more spreadsheet consulting in my spare time, but I simply do not have the capacity. I also currently try to focus on side hustles that have potential to be more of a passive form of income, not ones that require trading your time for a set amount of money.

6) FREELANCE WRITING

Freelance writing is one of those side hustles that everyone and their mother wants to get into. After all, who wouldn't want to sit at home all day sipping coffee and writing?

Unfortunately, this is the very reason why freelance writing is such a competitive field. The benefit of freelance writing as a side hustle is that you are not dependent on the income. You don't "need" to take on every job you get offered, nor is losing a client as devastating as it would be if it was your full-time income.

I was able to land a couple of freelance writing jobs through my blog. I had a fairly high minimum I charged per article and could have taken on additional jobs at a lower rate, but because it was my side income I was able to be picky and only take higher-paying jobs.

7) ENTERING GIVEAWAYS

Many people are surprised when I mention that entering giveaways was a side hustle of mine. They don't believe "winning things" is a real way to make money. Nevertheless, over the course of a two year period my wife and I entered thousands of giveaways. We even had a Friday "Giveaway Roundup" post on my blog during that time where we listed 100-300 giveaways that ended within the next week.

We were able to make some good money winning random things such as a car seat, a kitchen sink, a kid's bookshelf, a $400 lawn mower, tickets to the MLB All-Star game, countless gift cards, and many other things. We sold virtually everything we won and were able to turn it into a legitimate side hustle.

I still enter some of the bigger giveaways. I think it is worth your time to spend a few minutes here and there putting your name in the hat. You never know!

8) RENTING PART OF OUR HOUSE

My wife and I bought a house a few years ago that has a basement apartment and have rented it almost the entire time we've had the house. It's been a great side hustle, as the additional income has helped make owning a home more affordable.

Rental income is by no means a 100% passive income source, as we've put in a lot of work before, during, and after tenants have lived there. Having that monthly rent check, though, has made it well worth our time, especially since we are always looking for new ways to create side income sources to help pay down debt.

As you now know, I've tried many different side hustles. Hopefully you agree that nothing in this list is too out of the ordinary – I did not start a company that sold for millions nor did I invent a brand new product that is being sold all over the world. You do not need to do anything extreme or innovative to side hustle – it can be as simple or complex as you want it to be.

More likely than not, you have a few ideas of side hustles you think you'd enjoy pursuing, but will only be able to pursue one or two of those ideas due to limited time. The beauty of side hustles is that they allow you to pay off debt faster, save and invest money faster, and ultimately allow you to prioritize and pursue side hustles that may be riskier (i.e. launching a business that likely won't be profitable for more than a year) but offer potentially greater reward (sell the business for $10 million!).

The Pre-Hustle Checklist

Chapter 2

W hen it comes to the topic of how best to improve your financial situation, there are two camps in the personal finance world. The first camp believes cutting expenses and living a more frugal life is the best approach, while the second camp believes increasing income is the best approach. Most people fall somewhere in between these two extremes.

While this book is primarily focused on increasing income, it would be foolish not to look at some of the other ways to improve your finances before taking the side hustle route. After all, there may be some easy and practical ways to improve your finances that you haven't tried.

It's best to consider these options before starting a side hustle because once you start a side hustle it can be difficult to find the time or energy to pursue them.

In this chapter, we'll focus on three things: your current full-time job, your current financial situation (such as spending habits & debt), and your capacity to take on a side hustle.

FULL-TIME JOB: ARE YOU MAXIMIZING VALUE?

This book is all about making money in addition to your full-time job, so what's the point of talking about your 9-5? There's one important reason to first focus on your 9-5: it may be considerably easier to make more money at your 9-5 than it will be to make money at a side hustle.

Let's use an example to illustrate this point. Claire works 20 hours a week, every week, trying to make money blogging. Claire may spend 6-12 months making absolutely nothing, and then $500 a month, and finally $1k+ a month. Even when Claire reaches the $1k+ a month level, the income can vary and still requires Claire to sacrifice significant amounts of her spare time to keep the income coming in.

Let's say Claire works as a Marketing Analyst at a large corporation for her full-time job. Claire doesn't mind the work and has had good reviews the past two years. She's pretty comfortable in her current job and likes the people she works with. Plus she stays busy with her blog and has been making some money on it, so she's not in a huge rush to take on a new job with a new team.

So she waits.

And waits.

What should Claire do? What would you do?

Let's assume Claire is qualified for the next level at work. She's "due" as some would say, and could relatively easily find a Senior Marketing Analyst job. Let's also assume the increase in pay would be an additional $10k a year.

I think you see where I'm going with this.

If Claire was to start applying and interviewing for jobs at the next level, she would likely land one within a month or two. Let's also assume she wouldn't work longer hours. Sure, she may have more responsibility, but in many corporate jobs – especially at non-executive levels – most people work similar hours regardless of whether they are at entry level or middle management. By moving up, she would be making more money but would not need to sacrifice any additional time.

Getting a job at the next level would simply compound the impact of her side hustle. She would be bringing in more from her full-time job while still bringing in the same amount from her side hustle. She can continue to direct her side hustle towards debt and use the increase in her full-time income for savings, travel, or whatever she desires.

There are many work situations where you will know that you should be getting paid more. But how do you know for sure? I recommend every employee should regularly do two things: look at job openings and check GlassDoor for salary data.

LOOK AT JOB OPENINGS

One thing that I do at least once every month or two is look at job openings for the next level at work. I look at what types of skills fall into the required section and which fall into the preferred section. I see what sort of credentials and background knowledge hiring managers are looking for. I look at what technical and soft skills they desire.

I don't simply consume this information. I turn it into actionable items. If a majority of the jobs are looking for people who have worked with data, I would consider volunteering for projects that require me to query and analyze large data sets. I may even spend time outside of work building these skills (preferably through a side hustle).

I think everyone should regularly look at job openings for positions well before they actually plan on pursuing a new job. This provides time for the building up of skills and gaining the relevant experience that employers are looking for.

The biggest upside of looking at job openings is that there is a chance you may realize that you are qualified for a higher-paying job.

CHECK GLASSDOOR FOR SALARY DATA

One website that I recommend people visit at least once every few months is GlassDoor. GlassDoor has massive amounts of salary data as well as reviews of companies by both current and former employees.

The way GlassDoor works is it allows users to initially browse the site, but eventually prevents them from viewing additional information until they register and voluntarily offer up their salary information. There is no risk in offering up salary information because the data they display to the public is completely anonymous and aggregated.

GlassDoor can be extremely valuable to employees who are unsure whether they are getting paid a market rate. For example, I work in the finance department at a large corporation. As you can imagine, there are many people at the same level with the same title as me. On GlassDoor I can see the range of reported salaries as well as the average. If I'm getting paid $5,000 less than the average, I can confidently speak to my manager about moving my salary closer to the average.

You can browse tons of companies on GlassDoor and even filter for your specific geographic region. You may even find out that a comparable position at another company pays significantly more than your company. If so, it might be time to look into a move.

Frequently looking at job openings and doing salary research is not conventional advice, and most people only do it when they think they are ready to apply and interview for a new job. Don't be that person! Also, make sure you regularly update your resume and LinkedIn. You never know when an opportunity will come your way.

In a perfect scenario, you will be able to increase the amount of money you make at your 9-5 and then start a side hustle to increase your income even further. Increasing your 9-5 income isn't always possible, though, or may be limited based on tenure, company policy, and the type of work you do.

If you're maxed out from a compensation standpoint at your 9-5 but still desire a higher income, a side hustle is a great option for increasing your income.

ELIMINATE WASTEFUL SPENDING

While this book is focused on making more money to tackle debt and live a better life, it's essential to at least spend some time reviewing and reflecting on spending habits before making the decision to start a side hustle.

To illustrate this, let's use Ted as an example. Ted is a young professional who lives and works downtown. He spends about $1,500 a month renting an apartment in a trendy neighborhood. He also typically eats out for most meals – not to mention frequent happy hours.

Despite having a good job for a 20-something, Ted is struggling to pay his $800 monthly student loan bill on top of all his other expenses.

Now let's say Ted decided to review his spending. For two months, he recorded all his spending and put it into a spreadsheet. He was shocked to find that he spends over $1,000 on restaurants and drinks each month. Plus his rent and utility costs were making up a large portion of his spending. He wasn't saving or investing much and was truly living paycheck to paycheck.

Reflecting on this news, Ted decides to move to a suburb where there are more rental options and finds a one-bedroom for $800/month, significantly less than the $1,500/month he was paying downtown. He starts to bring a lunch to work and cuts back on how often he goes out to dinner.

Ted may be an extreme example, but the point is this: if you're struggling with debt, one of the first things to do is review your spending. Most people do not typically track their spending in great detail for two reasons: they are afraid at what they will find and it can be time-consuming.

Tracking your spending for a couple months and reviewing how much of your income is going to each spend category can be eye-opening for some. For others, there may be no surprises.

If there are areas you can cut back on, it likely makes sense to make the change. If you are committed to starting a side hustle, you may be able to increase your spending in those areas down the road. After all, side hustles should provide freedom so that you can choose to spend money on things that you would otherwise not be able to afford.

CHECK YOUR DEBT

Not all debt is equal. There is a big difference between high-interest credit card debt and low-interest mortgage debt. The interest rate on my mortgage is 3.5% and I plan on paying that loan off as slowly as possible, simply because I'm locked in at such a low rate.

Some personal finance gurus will tell you to pay off your debt regardless of the interest rate. I can respect this view if it comes from the perspective that the psychological benefit of being debt free outweigh the benefit of holding on to low-interest debt.

With that being said, I think there is a lot to be gained from holding low-interest debt and, instead of paying down debt faster, building up savings and investments. But that may be for another book. I highly recommend everyone with credit card debt or student loans take a closer look at the interest rate and their options for bringing their rate down and, in turn, bringing down the amount they pay towards interest.

CREDIT CARD DEBT

High-interest credit card debt can be debilitating. Even if you are determined to pay it down, there's a good chance that it will take more than a month or two to get rid of it, meaning you will continue to pay a large amount of interest instead of paying down the principle.

There are two approaches you can take to alleviate some of the pain of high-interest credit card debt. The first is to find a 0% APR credit card that you can transfer the balance to. These credit cards give you a grace period – typically 12 months – where you do not have to pay any interest on the balance you transfer over.

Having this breathing room can be a huge benefit to people who are struggling with credit card debt. Not only will it instantly free up some cash flow, it will also allow you the time to take other steps towards paying down the debt, such as working a side hustle.

0% APR card offers change often, so I won't recommend any specific cards at this time (you can always check Young Adult Money for up-to-date offers). If you do take this approach, keep in mind that some charge a one-time balance transfer fee to make the initial transfer.

The second option is to get a debt consolidation loan. The interest rates on these loans will not be rock-bottom, but they have potential to bring the rate down from 20%+ to something like 10% (and sometimes even lower). A credit card with a 0% APR transfer is the best option but if you don't qualify for one, a debt consolidation loan may be a good secondary option.

STUDENT LOAN DEBT

I think everyone who has student loan debt is well aware of the harsh reality that there is no magic formula for getting rid of it. While I think having a side hustle can greatly improve your ability to pay down student loans, it's worthwhile to discuss student loan refinancing³ before diving into side hustle strategies.

Student loan refinancing works similar to a mortgage refinance. A company pays off your loans and sets you up with another loan at a lower interest rate. The benefit to the loan holder is the potential for huge savings if they refinance at a significantly lower interest rate.

Student loan refinancing isn't for everyone, as you do lose some of the rights that come with student loans. One of those rights is being able to defer your loans when you are in grad school or if you face financial hardship. Be sure to take a look at these things before you decide to refinance.

---

3. You can find more information about student loan consolidation at http://www.YoungAdultMoney.com/StudentLoanRefi.

CAPACITY – HOW MUCH DO YOU HAVE?

Having the capacity for a side hustle is important. Side hustles are inherently difficult and draining because they are done on top of a full-time job. Burnout is a very real possibility.

When I think of capacity, I always think back to a talk that was given at a one-day leadership conference that I attended a few years ago. This leadership conference was focused on staff and volunteers of various non-profits. The speaker made a point about capacity that has stuck with me to this day.

Essentially what they said was that you need to be able to say "no" to things and create capacity for the things you prioritize. If you are going to start a side hustle, do you have enough free time to actually make it happen? Do you need to cut something out of your life to free up the time and capacity for your side hustle?

If your weekdays are already jam-packed from 6AM to 11PM, how are you going to make a side hustle work? Do you have time on the weekends that you can utilize for your side hustle? Are there other commitments you can scale back or eliminate altogether to create capacity for your side hustle?

I know someone who actually quit their full-time job practicing law because it allowed them little to no capacity to pursue a side hustle or even have much of a life outside of the office. It was assumed everyone would come in and work on Saturdays and there was a lot of pressure to put in more hours. She hated the work and culture so she pursued a 9-5 job that was truly a 9-5. This gave her capacity to pursue her side hustle and overall made her much happier with her work/life balance.

Knowing your priorities is extremely important. Yes, there are obligations to your full-time job, your family, and others, but ultimately, if you're committed to paying off debt through side hustles, you need to make them a priority.

Throughout running Young Adult Money the past three-plus years, I have had to sacrifice a considerable amount of time to write content, edit content, promote the site, and all the other things that go into running a successful blog. There were many nights and weekends that were spent at home or coffee shops putting in work. It's been difficult at times but being able to offset my monthly student loan payments – and then some – has made it totally worth it.

Even writing this book required me to sacrifice other opportunities. I was set to begin the part-time MBA program at the University of Minnesota when the opportunity to write this book came about. After careful consideration, it was clear that this book was a higher priority than starting my MBA. Luckily I was able to defer enrollment until the following semester.

Sacrifices for side hustles are often much smaller than delaying an MBA, though. It may mean getting a little less sleep on weeknights, or saying no to that second (or third) fantasy football league. Ultimately, if you are willing to make your side hustle a priority and recognize that it won't always be easy to fit into your schedule, you are far more likely to succeed than someone who went in blind without first considering the consequences.

Below is an actual checklist you can use to make sure you cover all your bases prior to pursuing a side hustle:

THE PRE-HUSTLE CHECKLIST

Looked into potential for a higher-paying job

- Are you qualified for a higher-paying job?
- Have you reviewed salary data on GlassDoor?

Tracked and reviewed income and expenses

- Tip: Use a free income/expense tracking spreadsheet[4] or program like Mint
- Where are you spending more money than you would like?

Lowered interest rate on debt where possible

- Will your creditors consider lowering your interest rate?
- Does a 0% APR card make sense? Is it an option for you?
- Does a personal loan make sense to consolidate high-interest credit?

Reviewed student loan payback options

- Can you lower your monthly payment through income-based repayment?

Now that we've finished the pre-hustle checklist, let's get on to the fun stuff – finding the right side hustle.

---

4. We have a free one on Young Adult Money that you can use: http://www.YoungAdultMoney.com/FreeExpenseTracker

Finding the Right Side Hustle for You

Chapter 3

T he good thing about side hustles is that there are a ton of options. The bad thing about side hustles is that there are a ton of options.

It's easy to get stuck in "idea land" when it comes to side hustles. Once someone starts thinking about starting a side hustle, it's not uncommon to think of multiple ideas they'd like to pursue. Having more options isn't a bad thing, but it becomes a problem if it prevents you from taking action and actually starting a side hustle.

I think the process for starting a side hustle is comparable to the process of starting a blog. There's an unlimited number of topics, an unlimited number of designs and an unlimited number of choices to make about a blog. A lot of people like the idea of starting a blog, but they don't actually ever execute their idea.

The most important part of a side hustle is actually getting started. This chapter is all about finding the right side hustle for you. It won't help you decide exactly which side hustle to start, but it will help you identify which type of side hustle best fits your lifestyle, personality, and interests.

Let's get started with what I think is the easiest way to categorize side hustles: "quick money" versus "long tail."

"QUICK MONEY" VERSUS "LONG TAIL"

The premise of this book is starting side hustles to pay down debt faster. Some people may be in a desperate situation where they need money ASAP. If you fall into this group, then you will be better off pursuing a "quick money" side hustle instead of a "long tail" side hustle.

Quick money is fairly self-explanatory: it's a side hustle that provides you with money fast. It is guaranteed side hustle income, and it starts as soon as you start your side hustle. One of the best examples of a quick money side hustle is delivering pizzas.

When I worked at a pizza shop in high school, there were a few drivers who only worked a couple of hours a night. They were people who had other full-time jobs but delivered pizzas on the side to supplement their income. They liked the consistent pay, the short weeknight shifts that fit in the hours outside of their

9-5, and the fact that the work was more physical than other 9-5s, such as programming.

There are countless quick money side hustles. They include:

- Working at a retail store nights/weekends
- Taking a seasonal job around the holidays
- Tutoring
- Mystery Shopping
- Product Demonstration
- Bartending

Quick money side hustles are ideal for people who want income that is guaranteed, do not want to start their own business, and are content with doing a different type of work than they do in their 9-5.

This contrasts with what I call "long-tail" side hustles. Long-tail side hustles do not guarantee income, typically require a more entrepreneurial mindset, and can potentially turn into more work than was originally anticipated. On the plus-side, long-tail side hustles offer a few unique potential benefits: the possibility of selling a business for a lump sum, the possibility of a new career, and the potential to bring in a lot more money long-term than a quick money side hustle.

Blogging is a classic example of a long-tail side hustle. Bloggers can go 6-12 months without making a dime, and may even end up losing money. There is no guarantee that a blog will ever make money. It also almost always takes more time and effort than people anticipate.

On the plus-side, a profitable blog can typically be sold for a lump sum. There is also the potential to have it morph into a full-time job, especially if the blog catches on and attracts readers. Blog owners can also leverage their site to get freelance writing and other "gigs." Finally, blogging can be great for entrepreneurs who want to manage a small business in their spare time. It requires managing content (the product), brokering advertisements, marketing, finances, and everything else that a business owner would encounter.

Blogging isn't for everyone and is definitely not the only long-tail side hustle option. Some other long-tail side hustle options are:

- Teaching music lessons
- Selling a product on Etsy
- Developing, manufacturing, and selling a product online
- Public Speaking
- Event Videographer
- Accounting for a small business
- Tax Preparation
- Starting a Podcast
- Become a YouTube personality
- Alterations/Tailoring
- Social Media Management

There is definitely a gray area when talking about quick money versus long-tail side hustles. For example, you could argue that tutoring is really a long-tail side hustle, as you need to establish yourself and build a reputation and, in turn, clientele. But you could also argue that tutoring is a quick money side hustle because there are companies that hire people to tutor for hourly rates, and there is little or no effort required to get clients.

Regardless of all the gray area that comes with categorizing side hustles as either quick money or long-tail, the focus should be on the side hustler instead of the side hustle. Going back to the tutoring example, it would make sense for someone who wants to build their own tutoring business on the side and/or have more control over their time and compensation to pursue the long-tail side hustle. If they need money quicker or simply want to put in the hours and get guaranteed money, they should instead pursue a tutoring position at an established company.

What we just described can be thought of in terms of the "ceiling" and "floor" of a side hustle. If you choose to deliver pizzas as a side hustle, you will likely get very consistent side hustle income. The ceiling, or the maximum you can make, won't be huge, but the floor, or the minimum you can make, also won't be that low. Essentially, you are trading a low ceiling for a predictable floor.

Now if you think about a side hustle that is more risk-based, such as having products manufactured in China and sold through a website you created, you will have a vastly different ceiling and floor than the person who chooses to deliver pizzas as their side hustle. The floor would actually be negative in this case, since you would have to invest thousands of dollars into your company without knowing whether you will even break even. The ceiling, though, is extremely high because it could turn into a company that generates lots of revenue and can be sold for a large amount of money.

I'll talk more about high-ceiling side hustles in the Unexpected Benefits of Side Hustles chapter, where I talk about funding riskier side hustles with stable side hustle income.

LOCATION-INDEPENDENT VERSUS LOCATION-DEPENDENT

Side hustles are no different than "regular" jobs or work in the sense that there are location-independent side hustles and location-dependent side hustles. Most people want to start a location-independent side hustle for the same reasons that many desire location-independent jobs: they don't want to deal with a commute, they want to work from the comfort of their home, and they want control over their environment.

I think everyone can imagine the benefits of having a location-independent side hustle, so instead I want to focus on the drawbacks that come with a location-independent side hustle. The biggest drawback is the higher level of competition. I will illustrate this with an example from my 9-5.

Before switching to my current 9-5 in corporate finance, I worked in corporate accounting. Despite the fact that we produce a virtual product and literally all the work is done on a computer, everyone still drives into a physical building to work each day.

While many of my colleagues were surprised when we started outsourcing work to our "Global Solutions" unit in India, I was not. Because the work could be done remotely, I knew that I was competing with people all over the world for my job.

Relating this back to side hustles, it's important to realize that with some location-independent side hustles you will end up competing with people all over the world, and sometimes it will make the side hustle not worth it. For example, I've considered doing more spreadsheet work as a side hustle, but it's tough competing with people overseas who are charging very little per hour.

It's worth noting that sometimes it's not so much the competition that forces people to quit location-independent side hustles, but the fact that they are not committed to putting in the work week-after-week without seeing consistent income from their efforts. Some things simply require more time and effort before they are successful. A podcast or Youtube channel could take many months to build up a sustainable audience.

Keep in mind that it can be beneficial to pursue a location-dependent side hustle if there is location-dependent work you enjoy. For example, there will always be demand for pet-sitting, house-sitting, dog-walking, landscaping, giving music lessons, food delivery, bartending, and other work that requires the person providing the service to be physically present.

One growth area ripe for location-dependent side hustles is anything related to the elderly/retired demographic. My grandparents have a caregiver who does many things for them that they can no longer do, such as going to the store for groceries and household items as well as well as tasks around the house like food prep and cleaning. The retired demographic also needs basic technology training. This is something that virtually any millennial can provide and is perfect for someone who has a lot of patience.

Another growth area ripe for side hustles is health and fitness. I know someone who gives group fitness classes in the evenings at a local gym. She enjoys leading the classes but does not do it as a full-time job. Personal training is another side hustle that health-conscious individuals might want to pursue. This could be turned into a location-independent side hustle if you create a website that has workout routines or videos showing people how to properly do certain exercises.

"SCHEDULED" WORK VERSUS "NON-SCHEDULED" WORK

One of the biggest benefits of a 9-5 is the predictable hours. Typically, day-after-day and week-after-week the hours are almost exactly the same. Income is predictable. At the same time, this can also be one of the biggest disadvantages of a 9-5, as some people work better late at night or are more productive if they work a few hours, take a few off, and then resume work.

Because side hustles are done in addition to 9-5 work, you have one big advantage: choosing whether to pursue scheduled or non-scheduled work. If you like having a definitive scheduled timeframe, there are many night and weekend jobs where you can work specific shifts. On the flip side, if you prefer to work whenever you want to - and not work when you don't want to - a side hustle like freelance writing might be ideal. Finally, there are some side hustles that have a mixture of both, such as a photographer who has scheduled photo shoots but can edit photos whenever (and wherever) they want.

So which is better? Scheduled or non-scheduled work? As with most things related to side hustles, the answer is "it depends."

Scheduled work is typically easier to find and more predictable (there's a reason 9-5 jobs are scheduled). If you need side hustle money ASAP and need it to be as consistent and reliable as possible, you almost certainly will want to look for scheduled work.

Work that does not have to be done during specific hours will inevitably be less predictable from an income standpoint, but it also may be more enjoyable work. One reason I love running a blog as a side hustle is because I can literally do it whenever I want. Yes, there is more competition than some other side hustles and revenue can be unpredictable, but I like being able to work on it when I feel like working on it.

Another question that comes up is whether a product or service is better. If you have the time and commitment to develop a product to sell, it may be a better option than providing a service. A good example of this is Janet Kim of Savvy Spreadsheets. She sells spreadsheets she has developed on her website SavvySpreadsheets.com. The nice thing about her side hustle is that she was able to develop the spreadsheets on her own time and does not need to be physically present when a customer purchases her spreadsheets – the whole sales and delivery process is automated through her website.

If you are pursuing a more entrepreneurial side hustle, I would encourage you to be open to both types of work. Janet also offers spreadsheet consulting services. While this may require her putting specific time on her calendar to meet with clients, it's just one more way to increase and diversify the revenue of her side hustle.

Another good example of a side hustle that can be either scheduled or non-scheduled is resume and cover letter consulting. Some people are naturally good at formatting and wording resumes and cover letters. This could be either a scheduled or non-scheduled side hustle. It would be scheduled if half-hour or hour-long meetings were set up with clients to review and improve their resume and cover letter. It would be non-scheduled if you simply have clients submit their resume and cover letter and they are reviewed and returned as time allows.

In general, if your goal is to make money ASAP to start padding your bank account and paying down debt, consider a side hustle that has scheduled work. If you have some breathing room and are able to deal with fluctuating and unpredictable income, consider looking into a side hustle that does not operate on a set schedule.

HOW YOUR LIFESTYLE & RELATIONSHIPS COME INTO PLAY

Throughout this chapter, one thing should have become clear: the side hustle you choose must fit with your lifestyle and current financial situation. If you're a husband and father, it's simply not realistic to have a side hustle that keeps you away from your family every weeknight or every weekend. If you're single, though, it becomes an option.

For one of my father's recent birthdays, we went to a restaurant to celebrate. As we were chatting with the waiter, we found out that he waited tables on nights and weekends on top of owning a landscaping business. Between the two jobs, he worked from 7am to about 10pm nearly every day. I assumed he was single because, let's face it, that sort of work schedule is only realistic if you do not have family commitments.

If you have a significant other and/or children, a little creativity can go a long way when it comes to side hustles. One strategy is to integrate your family into your side hustle. For example, while my wife is relatively hands-off with Young Adult Money, she has contributed blog posts in the past and even put together a weekly giveaway post every week for two years.

I have another friend who has a photography side hustle. His wife now second-shoots with him at weddings. Having your significant other work with you makes it a little easier to justify sacrificing summer weekends to work on a side hustle. In fact, I know a few photographers who have tried this arrangement and it can work well.

It's not just family and relationship demands that can make it difficult to work a side hustle. Many people have social, volunteer, education, hobbies, travel, and other commitments that make it difficult to sustain a side hustle.

There is no avoiding the work that comes with a side hustle. Even if you are able to build a business that is location-independent and that can be done on your own time, there will always be work that has to be done if you want to continue to make money at your side hustle.

Don't try to think of the side hustle that will be the least possible work because you will probably end up disappointed at how much more work it is than you thought. Instead, think of what fits best with your lifestyle and consider getting creative to make your side hustle work with your current responsibilities and commitments.

As you decide which side hustle to pursue, keep in mind that you can always stop and start a side hustle. After all, a side hustle should be at least somewhat enjoyable since you are sacrificing your free time to do it.

Don't be discouraged if you are currently in the camp that needs to pursue a side hustle that provides income immediately but wish you were able to pursue a long tail side hustle. You can always switch side hustles when your financial situation improves, which is inevitable if you are motivated enough to pursue a side hustle in the first place.

Use the following worksheet to help you get started with finding the right side hustle for you.

CHOOSING THE RIGHT SIDE HUSTLE

List 3 of your hobbies

1. _____

2. _____

3. _____

List 3 of your skills

1. _____

2. _____

3. _____

QUESTIONS:

Can I do a side hustle related to my hobby? What would that look like?

_____

_____

_____

What problem can I solve for people using my skills?

_____

_____

_____

How can I provide value to others?

_____

_____

_____

Do I need money ASAP or would it make more sense to pursue a side hustle that may take longer to be profitable?

_____

_____

_____

Do I need to pursue a location-independent side hustle or am I open to a location-dependent side hustle? How important is this to me?

_____

_____

_____

Do I need to pursue non-scheduled work or am I open to scheduled work? How important is this to me?

_____

_____

_____

List 3 side hustle ideas that sound appealing to you

1. _____

2. _____

3. _____

Part

Side
Hustle
Ideas

Quick Cash
Side Hustles

Chapter 4

S o far we've been focused primarily on preparing to start a side hustle. Preparation is key, but what about ideas for specific side hustles?

Over the next few chapters, we will explore several ideas for side hustles. These side hustles range greatly by type. Some are location-independent while others require being physically present. Some will virtually guarantee consistent side income, while others are potentially more lucrative but may not pan out.

There is some overlap in the bucketing of side hustles, but I did my best to put the side hustles into logical categories based on what people are looking for in a side hustle. Some may need cash quickly, so the quick cash side hustles section will give them ideas of side hustles that will accomplish this. Others may only desire a work-from-anywhere online side hustle. The online side hustles section will be where they want to look.

There is a side hustle for everyone. There are literally thousands of opportunities for side hustles. These are a few ideas to help with your own brainstorming.

We'll start by talking about quick cash side hustles. The ones that offer the quickest cash typically involve getting a part-time job. Taking on a part-time job in addition to a full-time job can start bringing in cash flow as quickly as a couple weeks.

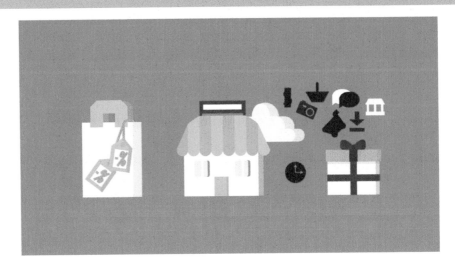

Working a retail job is one of the quickest and easiest ways to make side hustle money. There are countless retail stores in any given city with a huge variety of atmospheres, hours, and needs. There is also high turnover in retail so there typically won't be a long interview/onboarding process.

Retail could be an easy way to work just a few hours a week, such as a Saturday shift or a couple weeknight shifts. It can be very accommodating to those who desire to work strictly evening or weekend shifts. Plus people are typically looking to get rid of hours so there is always an opportunity to add more hours if you want.

FOOD DELIVERY

Food delivery, like retail, is an industry that is perfect for people looking to supplement their income. It may not be the most glamorous thing to do in your spare time, but there is always demand for qualified drivers to work in the evening and weekend hours.

My first job was cooking at Pizza Hut and I also worked at a pizza shop that is local to Minnesota called Davannis. At Pizza Hut in particular, drivers made more money than the managers. Delivery drivers also are needed most during dinner rush, so there is potential to work just 2-3 hours at a time and collect some decent side income.

WAITING TABLES

My sister waited tables for a couple summers in addition to her full-time job. There is a restaurant in Minnesota that is located on Lake Minnetonka that typically attracts wealthy customers. Sometimes she made more money in her short night shift than she did at her 9-5.

Waiting tables isn't easy. It can be stressful, tiring, and frustrating. It can – and will – be worth it, though, if you are focusing on debt repayment and other financial goals.

Like waiting tables, bartending is another service industry job that will always be in demand. There are countless restaurants that need servers and bartenders, typically in the evening and weekend hours that are prime for people looking to side hustle.

Restaurants and retail aren't the only industries that offer accommodating side hustle part-time job opportunities. To give a few examples:

OFFICE/CUBICLE MOVER

As I mentioned earlier, I had a part-time job as an office/cubicle mover. The shifts were Friday nights and Saturday mornings, but only when I wanted to work.

CHILD CARE

My wife worked at the YMCA for over a decade. She reached this incredible milestone by simply never quitting her part-time job in Kid's Stuff. She continued to work on Saturdays throughout college and even for a few years after college. It was a nice side income source and the fact that she enjoyed the work was a big bonus. We were also able to get a free gym membership through her employment. Just another way to cut monthly costs.

CONCESSIONS AT A SPORTS STADIUM

Professional sports offer a wealth of side hustles, from sports writing to jobs at the stadium. I have a number of friends who have worked in concessions in their spare time at MLB games, as well as one friend who covers Minnesota sports as a freelance writer.

If you want quick, predictable, stable side income, part-time jobs can be a great option. They may not be as glamorous as some other side hustles, but they do oftentimes allow more flexibility and options than most people think.

PRODUCT DEMONSTRATING

Being a product demonstrator can be great for anyone looking for a side hustle that has predictable pay and doesn't require as much mental energy or effort as other side hustles, such as starting a freelancing business. It is also ideal for someone not looking to take on a part-time job and prefer to not be constantly monitored by a manager. You've probably seen product demonstrators at various retail stores on the weekend.

Chonce from the blog My Debt Epiphany was a product demonstrator for three years and she thinks this is one of the best side hustles out there. Starting pay is around $11-$13/hour and can be as high as $20/hour. Shifts typically last between 4 and 8 hours. It's realistic to make $300-$500 in side hustle money every month.

While some retailers hire product demonstrators to work in their stores, other retailers work with a company that specializes in product demonstrations. Liquor stores are a popular place for product demonstrations, for obvious reasons. My sister did wine demonstrations in the past and enjoyed the work. It's also worth noting that alcohol product demonstrators typically make more per hour than other product demonstrators.

MYSTERY SHOPPING

Mystery shopping is another good way to make money on the side without having to take on a part-time job. Some people actually find shopping fun and would jump at the opportunity to be paid to do it – I know, it's difficult for some of us to understand!

Mystery shopping is relatively straightforward. Companies want feedback on their customers' shopping experience. To get that data, they are willing to incentivize shoppers to give their feedback. Cue mystery shoppers.

Once established, you can do as many or as few mystery shops as you want. Kristin from the blog Believe in a Budget says that those who take it seriously can make a few hundred dollars a month up to a couple thousand a month. Kristi recommends MysteryShopForum.com for finding out more about mystery shopping and iSecretShop.com for getting shops.

The shops can vary in type. They can include eating at a restaurant, checking out a new apartment complex, going to a health spa, viewing a movie, or any number of other things.

DONATING PLASMA

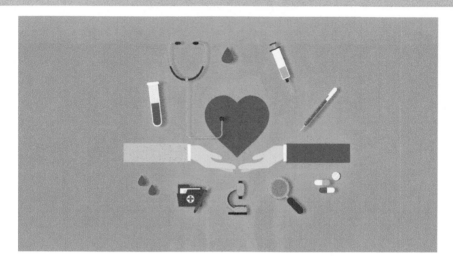

Probably the most well-known side income source is donating plasma. Plasma is the protein-rich part of the blood that carries red and white blood cells. Plasma is necessary for treatment of a number of rare diseases.

The amount of money you can make donating plasma varies. It can range from the low end of $10 per donation all the way up to $60 per donation. The first visit typically takes around two hours as a health exam is necessary, but after the first visit it should only take an hour to an hour and a half.

The Food and Drug Administration allows people to donate blood/plasma twice per seven-day period. If you have tattoos you may not be able to donate. Many donation centers are open later in the evening (i.e. until 8pm) so it works well for people looking to donate in addition to a 9-5 schedule. An added bonus is you are (literally) saving lives by donating plasma. It can take hundreds of plasma donations to make medicine to treat one patient for a full year.

CAREGIVING & SENIOR SERVICES

As mentioned earlier, there is a lot of demand for services for senior citizens. As more and more baby boomers retire, there will continue to be an increased demand for services for senior citizens. Providing services on the weekend or evenings is an option, as it could give full-time caregivers a break, or provide minimal services to senior citizens who are more independent.

Running errands like getting groceries and household goods can help elderly individuals stay in their own home. Additionally, services like cleaning, food prep, laundry, and providing transportation are all things that elderly individuals may need.

As a caregiver you could provide specialized services, such as only grocery delivery. Having just one service would allow you to batch the work, such as only making one grocery store run but shopping for three or more customers. Keep in mind other things that seniors may need, such as computer training or help integrating new technologies into their home like internet service.

Online Side
Hustles

Chapter 5

Online side hustles are side hustles that can be done anywhere there is an internet connection. Online income has definitely been put on a pedestal for the past decade because, well, who wouldn't want to make money from the comfort of their own home?

With that being said, it's important to be realistic when it comes to online income. It can be difficult to compete with others for online income simply because it's such a desirable way to make money.

However, it is absolutely possible to make money online if you are motivated enough. After all, nearly 100% of my side hustle income the past few years has come from online side hustles.

BLOGGING

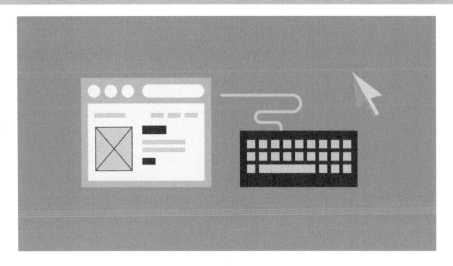

Blogging[5] has been my primary source of side hustle income the past three years and I've blogged off and on for nearly a decade. Blogging is an ideal side hustle because you can work on it whenever you want, it can be done anywhere you have an internet connection, you don't have to work with anyone you don't want to work with, and it's easy to start and stop whenever you want.

As I said earlier, I started Young Adult Money in July 2012 with the goal of making enough money to offset our $1,000/month student loan payment. Since then, I've reached and surpassed that goal, and have met many other bloggers who have been successful at turning blogging into a side hustle. It can be done.

There are some downsides to blogging. Sometimes I've referred to blogging as "the content rat race" because there are so many websites out there putting out similar content. It's a constant battle to provide value and get people to your site. It can take 6-12 months of hard work getting your blog established before you make any money from it. Despite the downsides, if you are dedicated enough, you have a good chance of making side hustle money through your blog.

Blogging comes with a lot of upside, which is why I think it makes for a good side hustle. A friend of mine was on ESPN for a panel about a Daily Fantasy Sports scandal because he was identified as an expert due to his Daily Fantasy Sports blog. You never know where blogging will take you.

5. If you'd like to pursue blogging as a side hustle, go to http://www.YoungAdultMoney. com/StartABlog for a guide on how to get started.

SELLING ON ETSY

Etsy is an e-commerce marketplace where people can buy and sell handmade or vintage items and supplies. Etsy does allow unique manufactured goods as long as they fall under what they define as "unique," such as utilizing a cut-and-sew shop to make clothes you've designed.

Technically, selling on Etsy can't be done from anywhere since it would be impractical and cost prohibitive to ship your products from, say, the Philippines, but it can be done from the comfort of your home.

Many people have built successful side hustles from Etsy. One example is Jennae Olson and Liz Carr, who started the Etsy business Walkin on Air that specializes in unique wedding shoes and other wedding-related items. They have nearly 9,000 sales as of this writing.

One thing to keep in mind with Etsy is that sales can start slow. It took Jennae and Liz two years before they started to bring in decent income from their shop, but that was primarily because they re-invested their earnings.

When I talked to Jennae, she stressed the need to have products that set your shop apart. In her words, "I think many times people try to sell products that are already oversaturated on Etsy. If there are already several shops selling products similar to yours and you are unable to differentiate your product from theirs, you will find yourself with too much competition. If your item looks very similar to someone else's, many times a customer will choose the cheaper item."

VIRTUAL ASSISTANT

Virtual assistants do all sorts of work for business owners. From answering emails to keeping track of and processing financials, there is a long list of things that a virtual assistant can do.

If you are looking to be a virtual assistant as part of a side hustle, you'll want to find a business owner who will allow you to put in hours outside of the traditional 9-5 workday. While some may want their virtual assistant to respond to emails throughout the day, others will be flexible and allow you to complete work as you have time.

One thing to keep in mind if you want to become a virtual assistant is that there are inexpensive options overseas for virtual assistants. Some virtual assistants will work full-time for as little as $500 a month. With that in mind, be sure to point out how you differentiate yourself from an overseas virtual assistant, perhaps by pointing out your ability to take on higher-level tasks, ability to work with less direction, the fact that English is your first language, etc.

Social media management is a service many virtual assistants offer, but it can also be a stand-alone service offering. Some people even offer management of a specific social media channel, like Pinterest.

There is a huge need for effective social media management among brands and small businesses. Many businesses have either not prioritized social media or do not manage it optimally. Some brands simply don't enjoy running social media so they do the bare minimum. If someone was to offer them social media management for a reasonable fee there is a good chance they'd take them up on it.

To get started in social media management it makes sense to offer free services to gain some experience and a client (or clients) to reference to future prospects. A bulk of the work behind social media management can be done through tools like Buffer or Tailwind, which allows you to schedule social media postings, effectively making it a side hustle that is location-independent and not scheduled.

FLIPPING THINGS ON EBAY OR CRAIGSLIST

Flipping things on eBay or Craigslist is another "online" side hustle that can be lucrative for someone who is good at spotting deals and likes dealing with physical products as opposed to something that is entirely virtual.

There are a number of bloggers I know who have talked about flipping things on eBay and Craigslist. It works like this: first, you find something for cheap or free at a garage sale, thrift store, or on the side of the road. You fix it up or refinish it, and then list it for sale on Craigslist or eBay.

Simple enough?

Some people take this to the next level and try to make a full-time income out of it. One of my parent's neighbors refinishes furniture as a full-time job. She is constantly buying and selling furniture and has perfected the craft with a system that works for her.

Graphic design can be done entirely online and opens up the door to many potential customers regardless of where they are located.

With virtually every single company being present online, there is huge demand for graphic design work. Every small business needs great branding and great design, not to mention the countless mid-size and large businesses. Companies also are constantly rebranding, creating a steady, never-ending stream of demands.

I talked to Amanda Wahlund, who is now a full-time freelance graphic designer, about her experience doing graphic design as a side hustle. Pro-bono work is a good way to build a portfolio while also getting exposure and building a network of potential clients. Additionally, she wishes she had spent more time building up her side hustle business before becoming a full-time freelancer. Getting a great website and getting a larger base of paying customers are two ways that can be accomplished.

There is a lot of competition for graphic design due to sites like Elance. I posted a job for a new logo for Young Adult Money and received 27 offers within 24 hours. Even with that in mind, people will almost always prefer hiring contractors who were referred to them. If you can start with a few clients and build a solid reputation, you will always have a growing number of potential clients.

CREDIT CARD CHURNING

Credit card churning is the process of signing up for credit cards to get a sign-up bonus and then subsequently closing the cards once you have used the bonus. It's a way a lot of people travel for cheap or free. I think of it as a side hustle because you are "making" money in the process of signing up and closing cards.

To give you an example, there was a credit card that offered a $400 travel credit that can be used on any travel expense as long as you signed up for the card and charged at least $3,000 on it within 3 months. It has an annual fee, but it's waived for the first year. So if you shift as much of your spending as possible to the card and hit the $3,000 required spending, you get the $400 credit. Other cards offer miles or even cash-back.

It goes without saying that you should only churn credit cards if you have no credit card debt, are able to fully pay off your credit card bill each month, and do not spend unnecessarily to get the credit card rewards. Before getting started, you should also look into how frequently closing cards will affect your credit both in the short- and long-term.

OPINION-GIVER

Filling out surveys is one of the oldest ways to make money online, and marketers' desire to get consumer's opinions on future products hasn't slowed down at all.

One warning I would give if you decide to pursue this as a side hustle is that there are a lot of spammy sites out there that really aren't worth your time. A few of the more legitimate sites are:

- UserTesting
- 20/20 Panel
- Harris Poll
- Nielsen Digital Voice

One thing to be clear about is that you will not make a ton of money filling out surveys or giving your opinion. This can be a good side hustle to couple with other side hustles, like mystery shopping or even a part-time job.

PODCASTING

Like blogging, podcasting can be a lucrative location-independent side hustle. There are a number of people who make a part-time or full-time living through podcasting. If you are able to establish a podcast and build a sizable audience, there will almost certainly be advertisers in your niche that are willing to sponsor episodes.

Similar to how freelance writing or blogging can lead to new opportunities, podcasting can lead to new opportunities or even a new career. Podcasters have experience in audio production as well as in building an audience. They are relatively safe bets for companies looking to hire or contract out media production.

There are a couple of reasons why people fail at making a side hustle out of podcasting. First, people struggle getting those key first listeners. It's easier to market a podcast if there is already a blog or some sort of social media presence established. Second, people seem to quit too early. Podcasts are like blogs – they take a long time to establish. Quitting after three, four, even ten podcasts seems to be fairly common in the podcasting community.

CREATING YOUTUBE VIDEOS

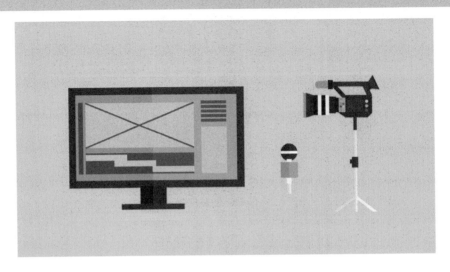

YouTube has been around for a while now and you likely have heard rumors of people that make millions a year creating YouTube videos. While YouTube doesn't release how much specific YouTube channels generate, it's widely known that there are YouTubers who make in excess of $100k a year off of advertising revenue.

I'm jealous of anyone who is able to produce good video content. I'm not skilled in the area, but I do think it's the most lucrative media avenue to pursue. Recently, companies like Facebook have been moving into the video space and video producers are able to leverage the competition for better advertising rates.

Besides publishing YouTube videos and making money off of advertising, there are also many people (like myself) who would like video content for their website/brand/company but do not have the skills to do so. If you can create quality videos on YouTube, you immediately have a portfolio of your work, making it more likely that you will be hired for freelance work. If you have video skills and some ideas for a YouTube channel, it's a great path to pursue for side income, especially due to the potential upside of contract video work.

Small Business Side Hustles

Chapter 6

There are many reasons someone would want to focus on a side hustle that has potential to turn into a full-time business. Perhaps they don't want to stay in their current job/career forever. Or maybe they like the idea of making a significant amount of money on the side to make early retirement a possibility.

Whatever the reasons, there are many side hustles that have potential to turn into a full-time business. In fact, many of the side hustles I've already mentioned, such as starting an Etsy business or a blog, have potential to grow into a full-time business.

In this section, I want to call out a few ideas and strategies for people specifically looking to start a side hustle that can grow into a full-time business. Again, keep in mind that there is some overlap with other sections, as these are not the only side hustles that have potential to turn into a larger business.

CREATING AN ONLINE PRODUCT TO SELL

If you're looking for passive online income, there is no better way to do it than to create an online product to sell. It requires none of the coordination of production and distribution that comes with a physical product, and it can literally make you money while you sleep.

One of the former writers for Young Adult Money, Cat Alford, created a training course for people looking to make money as a freelance writer. While Cat has a lot of demand for her writing services, this was a smart move for her because any money she makes off the course[6] is passive. She doesn't have to work x hours or produce x posts for a website owner. The course is created and people are purchasing and using it without any additional time commitment on her part.

Another great example is Savvy Spreadsheets. I recently purchased a spreadsheet on the site and loved the system that Janet set up. She is able to make passive income indefinitely off of spreadsheets she has already created. The sales and delivery process is online and entirely automated.

If you need money immediately, this may not be the route for you. But if you are okay financially and can sink some time into developing something to sell, this could be a smart way to go for the simple fact that you have a shot at creating a truly passive income stream.

6. You can see the course here: http://www.YoungAdultMoney.com/ FreelanceWritingCourse/

CREATING A PHYSICAL PRODUCT TO MANUFACTURE AND SELL

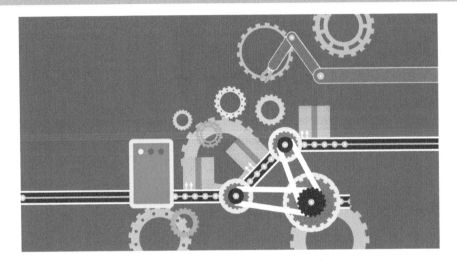

One book that has had a lasting impression on me is Timothy Ferriss' The 4-Hour Workweek. In the book he talks about "muses" which are essentially businesses based on a product that you create. The key to a successful muse is creating a system where you outsource every facet of it, from manufacturing, to order fulfillment, to customer service. This allows you to remove yourself as an owner and make passive income.

While I tend to prefer online products that do not require manufacturing, inventory management, or anything else that comes with a physical product, physical products do have a big advantage. They typically are not easy to replicate and there are far more barriers to entry than businesses that are based off of "virtual" products. There also are many companies that can take on various aspects of the supply chain and delivery process, allowing the owner to remove themselves and cash checks.

An example of a product that fits this description is EarPeace. EarPeace was created by Jay Clark and it aims to solve the problem of unattractive hearing protection. Per Clark,[7] "EarPeace is high fidelity hearing protection that turns down the volume without distorting the sound, it's virtually invisible, comfortable, reusable, and comes in fantastic packaging."

Another example is Square 36, an oversized yoga mat that Bob Maydonik created with a business partner. It solves the problem of regular yoga mats being too small and inadequate for workout programs like P90X.

Both of these entrepreneurs source their products from manufacturers they found on Alibaba, and are excellent examples of physical products that are unique and have a lot of upside. Not only does selling a physical product offer the potential for consistent, material, monthly income, but it also can potentially be sold down the road to an outside investor.

| 7. http://fourhourworkweek.com/2010/11/28/4-hour-work-week-case-studies-muse/

LAUNCHING A WEB-BASED SERVICE

Many web-based services have turned into billion-dollar companies. This is where you will find the Facebooks, Spotifys, and Ubers of the world. These services save people time and money, as well as connect people.

Some web-based services are straightforward. For example, eBay is a marketplace to buy and sell goods. Simple concept; complicated to implement. Not every web-based service needs to be a billion-dollar idea, though. Interestingly enough, most billion-dollar ideas don't seem that complicated (i.e. Airbnb's business model: coordinate short-term room, apartment, and house rentals).

Online services don't have to be a huge undertaking. You could start a web-based service that is simply a sole proprietorship that eventually grows into something bigger. Some content writing services started as one writer and grew into a business where tens or hundreds of writers were brought on to take on work. The same can be said about some tech consulting companies that started as small companies with one or two employees but eventually grew into much bigger businesses.

One example of a service-based online business is Excel Rain Main. Jen Portland started Excel Rain Man to help people and businesses with their Excel-related problems. She developed her skills at her full-time job and saw the potential to utilize her skills to provide Excel services to others. She now runs Excel Rain Man full-time and has a number of subcontractors that she delegates work to.

Jen's story illustrates an important point: if there is a particular skill that you have that is in demand in your workplace, there is a good chance that other individuals and companies have demand for that skill as well.

WEDDING-RELATED PRODUCTS & SERVICES

One industry that I think is ideal for side hustles is weddings. Weddings almost always happen at night and/or on the weekend. Many vendors are needed for every wedding, from music to catering to florists. There is also a ton of money in weddings and no sign of that trend slowing down.

Because there is so much demand in the wedding industry, there is also the potential for any given wedding side hustle to turn into a full-time business. A few wedding side hustles that could turn into full-time businesses are:

RENTALS

Chairs, decorations, linens, photo booths...you name it, there is a market for it.

PHOTOGRAPHY

Not just traditional photography, but also "photo booth" type photography.

COORDINATION

More and more weddings are having "day of" coordinators that make sure everything runs smoothly. This could also include wedding planning.

MUSIC

From DJ services to live music, both at the ceremony and reception.

OFFICIANT

If you enjoy public speaking and weddings, you can make a few hundred dollars for each wedding you officiate.

WEDDING-RELATED CLOTHING

Remember the business I mentioned in the Etsy section? They built a full-time business out of wedding shoes.

DECORATIONS

These can be custom-made decorations or gifts made specifically for a given wedding, both for purchase and rent.

There are many people who make a full-time living as wedding vendors. There is no limit to what these side hustles can grow into, especially for an entrepreneurial and business-minded individual. Even DJ services may seem like a one-man show, but our wedding DJ has built an entire business out of it and now has a number of employees working for and representing his brand.

ACCOUNTING & TAX SERVICES

Most sole proprietorships or even small businesses simply cannot justify a full-time accountant. This opens up an opportunity for those who work in accounting or tax full-time, as these businesses are likely to be more willing to hire someone who is only available on nights and weekends. If you enjoy tracking finances and keeping financial records, it can be a lucrative side hustle.

I've worked full-time as both an accountant and financial analyst, but even I have difficulties keeping up with the finances for my blog. Due to taxes it's not an option to not track my revenue and expenses, so either I have to do the work or I have to outsource it. Every other business owner is in the same situation. There are some people who target a specific niche, such as bloggers or Etsy store owners, and keep track of their finances for them.

Tax services are not limited to businesses, though, as there are many people who hire CPAs to fill out their tax forms for them. I know a number of people who do this as a side hustle during the busy tax season. It's a relatively sustainable side hustle, too, as there is a short period of time where it is extremely busy followed by many months of little to no work.

Self-Employment Side Hustles

Chapter 7

There are many people out there who are unhappy in their jobs and careers. They don't want to do it forever. They hate the commute, they dislike having little control over their schedule, and they want to be their own boss.

It can be very risky to quit a stable full-time job to pursue your dreams. Especially in today's economic climate where most students graduate with tons of debt, it's simply not an option for many.

The good news is that it's entirely possible to start a side hustle that will eventually turn into a self-employed career. One of the upsides to side hustling is the potential for becoming self-employed or a "solopreneur" as some like to call it.

Here are some ideas for side hustles that provide that upside.

FREELANCE WRITING

Nearly everyone knows how to write articles or blog posts (or can learn how to), and there seems to be an endless demand for new content. This makes freelancing a good side hustle starting point.

I've employed a number of freelance writers for Young Adult Money over the years and a few of them are freelance writers full-time. What I've noticed is that most freelance writers struggle to get started but once they are established it becomes easier to get jobs and charge more per hour.

So how do you get started in freelance writing? It helps to have a website or blog that showcases your writing. Once you have a website or blog, reach out to other blogs/content sites in your niche. Ask if they are looking to hire writers and, if not, offer to write a free guest post. This will help you get your first few freelance gigs and you can build from there.

It's important to not charge too much at first. Yes, writing for $10 or $20 a post doesn't sound desirable, but you can slowly increase.[8]

8. Check out http://www.youngadultmoney.com/FreelanceWriteSideHustle/ if you are interested in freelance writing as a side hustle.

WEB DEVELOPMENT

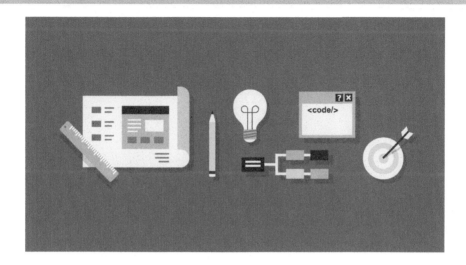

There is huge demand for web developers. Big companies need them, medium-sized companies need them, small companies need them and even sole proprietors need them.

Demand for web developers will not slow down because the number of brands, companies, and individuals who are looking for a positive web presence is constantly increasing. If you are good at web development, you will be able to find clients. Once you have a solid portfolio and references to back you up, the sky is the limit.

Web development is something that works well as a side hustle. You can spend 5, 10, or 30 hours a week working on it. Once you have enough demand, you can raise prices and be picky about which clients you work with and how much you charge.

Over the past couple of years, I've had a very difficult time finding a quality WordPress web designer. Almost every other blogger I've talked to has struggled to find a designer they were entirely happy with. I think this illustrates the void that exists that could be filled by quality designers, as well as the demand that is out there for web development skills.

DATABASE CONSULTING

With the huge amount of data that is available today, companies are struggling to keep up on the data management and data analysis front. While large corporations have millions of dollars to throw at data management, there are many small and mid-size companies that struggle with finding affordable solutions for their data needs.

Database consulting could be the ideal side hustle for you if you spend considerable time working with data in your full-time job. You may need to spend more time learning advanced database concepts. The last thing you want to do is suggest a solution to a client that doesn't work out because of your lack of skill or expertise.

It likely makes sense to do some free or low-compensation work for nonprofits or small businesses. Nonprofits and small businesses are most likely to be struggling on this front, as most established consultants and contractors charge a relatively high per-hour rate. You can use those first jobs as references for future gigs, not to mention that the owners or leaders you worked with may start referring other business owners your way.

PROGRAMMING

Programmers are in equally high demand today and will continue to be for the foreseeable future. Technology is being inserted into every area of our lives, and the trend is likely to continue. This trend represents a huge opportunity for people with coding skills.

Side hustle jobs are not difficult to find for a friend of mine who is a programmer. He's worked on a Daily Fantasy Sports (DFS) website where he was given equity in return for his work as well as a paid gig for a website that helps fill seats on private jets that would otherwise be sitting empty.

For the private jet website, the code was initially outsourced to programmers overseas, but my friend was brought in to clean up the code and do some of the more advanced coding.

One area within programming that may be ideal for programmers to focus on is app development. Nearly every company wants an app. There is also a lot of opportunity for app developers to create their own apps that bring in revenue or that they can sell to companies.

PHOTOGRAPHY

Do you like taking pictures? Photography may be the side hustle for you. I have a number of friends and acquaintances that have gone from doing photography as a side hustle to running a photography business full-time.

The reason photography is such a great side hustle is because there is a lot of demand for photography on nights and weekends. Families who want photographs typically need to schedule the shoot outside of their 9-5 jobs. Weddings are almost always on the weekend. Other events, like concerts or sporting events, typically take place in the evening.

Photography does have its downsides, though. If you are looking to turn it into a full-time job, you will have to continue the evening and weekend work schedule even after making the transition to full-time work, which isn't always desirable. Additionally, there is a lot of competition in this space, especially as cameras and technology make it much easier for even unskilled photographers to take "good" pictures.

With that being said, there is virtually unlimited demand for photographers. People will continue to get married and need photographers, events will continue to be scheduled where photographers are needed, and families will continue to desire family photo shoots. It's easy to slowly build up a large side hustle photography business and then make the switch to full-time work, if desired.

Photography is, in large part, referral based. This makes it essential to not overcharge when first starting out in the photography business. It may even make sense to do some work for free until you have built up a portfolio of examples for future clients. It goes without saying that having a website and social media presence will be key for roping in potential clients.

Most of what I said about photography can also be applied to videography. There is a lot of demand, especially in the wedding industry, for quality videographers. It's becoming more of a necessity than a "nice-to-have" for companies to produce and showcase video content tied to their brand. Even "solopreneurs" and individuals are looking to have videos created to improve their brand and set themselves apart from their competition.

Local Side
Hustles

Chapter 8

One of my favorite stories I like to share regarding the "remote" versus "required to be physically present" work debate involves a plumbing problem I had at my house. I was working in accounting at the time and was able to work remotely as needed. The plumber was doing his work and asked if I was working from home. I said yes, and he said that must be really nice to have that option.

While it is nice to have the option to work from anywhere, it also means I compete with hundreds of millions of people that my plumber doesn't compete with. In fact, around the time the plumber was over, we were in the midst of a round of outsourcing and I spent countless hours training people from India.

The plumber, on the other hand, will always have demand. Sure, he competes with other plumbing businesses in the area, but the competition is much more limited than competing against millions of people who can do your job overseas (for significantly less money, I might add).

In this chapter, I want to touch on what I call "local" or "neighborhood" side hustles. They are not side hustles that will be done online, nor are they side hustles that involve being employed by someone else. For the most part, they also fall short of having true potential of being a full-time job but I think this actually makes them even more attractive for people looking for a side hustle.

DOG WALKING

Is your full-time job outside of a regular 9-5 workday? Are you at home during the day? Most importantly, do you like pets?

If you answered yes to these questions, you might want to consider becoming a dog walker. According to Care.com, the average pay for a dog walker is $11.25/hour, but I've seen listings ranging from $10 to $30+ per 30-minute walk. You can sign up on Care.com to be a dog walker, as well as view job postings.

This is an ideal side hustle for someone who loves dogs and has a schedule that doesn't align to a typical 9-5. The reality for many working professionals is that they are gone longer than 8 hours a day. With both my wife and I working regular 9-5 jobs, we so far have decided against getting a dog, mainly because we would be unable to let them out during the day. That decision may change down the road if our income increases and we can justify hiring someone to walk our dog on weekdays.

There are many families that have decided to get a dog and are willing to pay someone to walk it in the middle of the day, or even in the morning or evening.

Anyone with a pet knows how difficult it can be to find someone to take care of it when they go out of town. If you are willing to take care of pets while people are out of town, you can make a nice side income with minimal effort. Thanks to the internet, it's become increasingly easy for pet owners to find people to take care of their pets, and vice versa. Websites like Rover. com, DogVacay.com, and Care.com are great places to list your services, availability, and experience.

While not exactly an apples-to-apples comparison, I do think pet care can be compared to freelance writing in the sense that you should charge less until you have a few positive reviews and some experience under your belt. Reviews and references are key!

Overnight or daycare for pets can net you anywhere from $20 to $100+ per night. The potential for income will vary depending on location, number and type of pets, and other factors. Pet care can work well for people who telecommute because it doesn't impact their 9-5 work schedule.

CHILD CARE

As I mentioned earlier, my wife continued to work at YMCA Kid's Stuff even after graduating from college. She would take Saturday shifts and only quit once she started grad school. While she said it can be stressful when there are too many kids at once, it was work she enjoyed and was a good source of side income.

While her work in child care was at an employer, there are opportunities for those in their 20s and 30s to watch kids on nights and weekends. There are two approaches that can be taken when pursuing child care as a side hustle, each with pros and cons.

The first is to make your intentions known as widely as possible. Even posting on Facebook that you are looking to babysit on the side might help you land a few jobs. The bonus in starting with people you know is that you are likely already familiar with the kids you will be watching. Once people are aware that you are looking to make some money on the side through child care, you will likely get some work through referrals. This could be a good side hustle for parents, too, as you already are watching kids so having additional kids to watch won't detract from your regular schedule.

The second approach is setting up a profile on a site like Care. com and getting leads that way. The benefit here is not needing to reach out to people you know, which could be awkward if you end up watching your friends kids, since there is a chance they may see it as a favor instead of something you should receive payment for.

RENTING SPACE

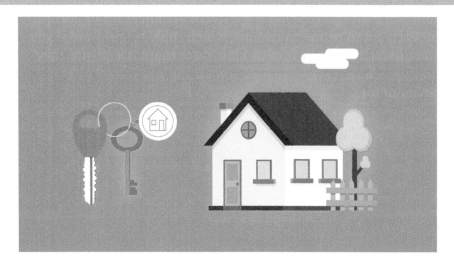

If you're looking to diversify your income and have some extra space in your home or apartment, it might make sense to get a roommate. Many college grads feel like it's their "right" to live alone and that they've earned it. But if you're struggling with student loan debt and have space that could be shared, it may be too big of a financial advantage to pass up.

Besides having a roommate, one thing that current and future homeowners may want to consider is the possibility of creating an apartment within their house. There are a couple things to keep in mind if you decide to go the space rental route. Always have a signed contract in place. There is a lot of risk in not having a contract and contracts set expectations for both parties. I also would recommend being picky when choosing who to share your space with. You want to have mutual trust and respect, so having someone move in who you already know will always be ideal.

Another approach to space renting that is becoming wildly popular is Airbnb. Airbnb is a website where you can list vacation rentals as well as find vacation rentals to book. As of this writing, there are more than 1.5 million listings in 34 thousand cities and 190 countries.

How much you can make will vary depending on city and what you are renting out. Some rentals are the entire apartment/ house, while others are just a bedroom or even a shared room. Many people are looking to travel for cheap and are willing to take a couch or shared room if it means they can save money. If you are comfortable welcoming others into your home and love being a host, this could end up being a great side hustle for you.

DELIVERY DRIVER

While the large majority of delivery drivers are employed by a company, there is more opportunity today than ever before for people to operate as independent contractors and work on their own schedule.

Uber is by far the best known "delivery" service, but it's not the only one. There are multiple startups such as Deliv and SpoonRocket that are trying to challenge the traditional delivery model.

The revolution in the delivery business is going to play in favor of those who are looking to spend a few hours a week delivering things as a side hustle. It's a win for everyone involved, as people do not have to commit to being an employee and the companies looking to have things delivered do not have to take on the financial risk of full-time employees.

If this side hustle sounds interesting to you, check and see if any of the delivery startups operate in your area and keep an eye out for companies that are expanding into new markets. The markets they serve may be limited now, but giant companies like Uber were also in just a few markets initially.

There will always be demand for tutors and teachers. Parents want their kids to be successful, and if that means paying someone to help them in an area of struggle, so be it.

If you are bilingual, this can be a particularly lucrative side hustle. Having the ability to speak more than one language is something that many parents seek for their children, and typically taking courses in school won't quite give someone enough exposure to become fluent.

I had a friend who gave guitar lessons throughout college. He was charging in excess of $50/hour, and parents were willing to pay his rate. He did this as a full-time job during college, but you can imagine how easy it would be to continue to give lessons on nights and weekends once he got a "regular" 9-5.

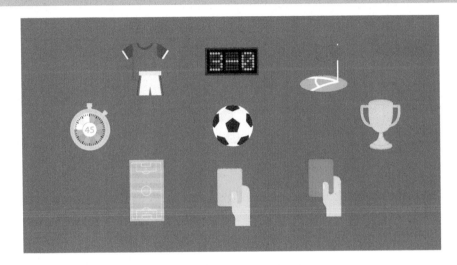

With how out of control youth sports has become (it's easy to be judgmental when you don't have kids of your own), there is a huge need for referees to officiate the never-ending tournaments and games that happen every single week of the year.

As with most things, how much you make will vary. Varsity and junior varsity games will pay more than youth games. I've heard that high school football will pay around $50 a game and soccer around $35 a game. Again, this will vary by city and state.

One thing to keep in mind is that youth and varsity sports are not the only demographics that need refs. There are lots of adult leagues that pay to have refs. For example, think of all the slow-pitch softball leagues that take place each summer and fall.

If you enjoy sports and think you will be able to deal with parents yelling at you, being a ref can be a great side gig. One of my former manager's husband refs high school football and, from my understanding, does it out of pure enjoyment– the side income is just a bonus.

COACHING SPORTS

Similar to the demand for referees, there is a lot of demand for coaches. Some coaching positions are unpaid, but many do compensate coaches for their time and effort.

Coaching can be a rewarding side hustle for a number of reasons. For many coaches, there is a satisfaction in helping develop people into better athletes and individuals. Coaching also allows former athletes to stay connected to a sport despite being past their playing days. Finally, many high school coaches receive a stipend for each season they coach, making it an ideal short-term side hustle with a definite start and end date.

A friend of mine coaches swimming at the YMCA once a week for an hour and a half. Not only does she get paid a little, but she also gets a free gym membership for her family. She also receives free child care while she coaches. Not a bad deal!

MEDICAL RESEARCH STUDIES

Medical research is a big field and, not surprisingly, those conducting the research need people to participate in the research. There are typically always research studies going on that compensate people for their time, especially if you have various medical ailments, such as asthma, diabetes, etc.

While I haven't sought out medical research studies, I did sign up and qualify for one related to asthma and allergies. The projected compensation is $900. The study hasn't started yet but I suspect it may end up being difficult to participate in with a regular 9-5 job, unless they have flexible hours.

I wouldn't recommend participating in medical research studies as a primary side hustle, but it can be a good way to make a little extra money from time-to-time, assuming you qualify.

When it comes to side hustles, the bigger a problem you can solve, the better. Moving is a huge headache and a stressful time for most people. This presents an opportunity for people who are willing to help make the experience a little less painful.

Many people prefer to move on the weekend, so the timing is ripe for a side hustle. Moving services could be as simple as charging per hour that you help or as complex as providing a moving truck/equipment and a small crew to make the move successful.

If you're able to lift more than the average person and don't mind doing some physical work each weekend, moving services can be an excellent side hustle. Increase your chances for success by establishing a formal LLC, write up contracts to protect yourself from potential damages caused in the process. The more professional you present yourself, the more at ease people to whom you provide your service will be.

Part 3

Side
Hustle
Better

Upside - The Unexpected Benefits

Chapter 9

The biggest reason I am a fan of side hustles can be captured in one word: upside.

Side hustles have potential for tremendous upside. Many businesses and second careers have started as a side hustle. One of my favorite examples of side hustles having huge upside is the comic strip Dilbert. Many people do not know that Scott Adams, founder of Dilbert, wasn't always a cartoonist. Dilbert started as a side hustle while Adams worked a 9-5.

As Adams describes in his book How to Fail at Almost Everything and Still Win Big, he tried many side hustles and businesses in his spare time prior to starting Dilbert. They included, among other things, creating computer games, a web video company, and a grocery home delivery service. Almost all either failed or were abandoned by him.

Through a combination of dedication, effort, luck, and timing, Adams succeeded in doing what most only dream of: turning a side hustle into a business that makes millions of dollars. The story of Dilbert is an inspiring one for anyone who is considering giving side hustles a try. Side hustles truly have the potential to change your life.

Most side hustles won't turn into million-dollar companies, but some will. Even taking a part-time job as a side hustle has potential upside, as you never know who you will meet or what ideas you will be exposed to in the process. Not to mention the fact that being proactive about paying down debt will naturally open up opportunities, since not having debt inevitably allows you to take advantage of more opportunities.

This chapter is all about the upside of having a side hustle. If you aren't already motivated to start a side hustle, you will be by the end of this chapter. If you already are planning on starting a side hustle, you will gain new perspectives and ideas of how you can best leverage a side hustle to better other areas of your life. Finally, I will touch on what I like to call "advanced side hustle potential" which is leveraging a side hustle to start another side hustle (it will make sense, trust me).

THE BENEFIT OF CONNECTIONS

Having a side hustle will naturally provide you with connections that you otherwise wouldn't have. These connections can lead to new (and better) jobs, new clients, and new business partnerships.

This is the biggest reason why I think everyone should have a blog or niche website about something they are interested in. A blog is an ideal side hustle because it makes it very easy to meet people and network. For example, with personal finance blogs there is an entire annual conference dedicated to personal finance bloggers. Many bloggers also comment on each other's posts, share articles, and in general are willing to help each other.

While it may take a while before your blog grows large enough to attract advertisers, simply having a blog will eventually bring in a regular flow of brands and companies who are interested in working with you. This can lead to opportunities that otherwise wouldn't be possible, such as advertising contracts, partnerships, and more.

For me, four opportunities came about solely from having a side hustle, and more specifically, a blog. They are:

POTENTIAL STARTUP CAPITAL

As I mentioned earlier, I used to work for a blog during college. I met the blog owner through my political blog. I've stayed in touch with him and I now broker advertisements for the multiple blogs he's acquired over the years.

Recently I've mentioned my desire to launch a business and he's expressed his interest in potentially supplying me with capital in exchange for equity in the company. Anyone who has tried to launch a business or raise money for a new business will tell you just how important a connection like this is.

SPREADSHEET SIDE HUSTLE

Remember Janet Kim, founder of Savvy Spreadsheets, who I mentioned earlier? I initially reached out to her to see if she was interested in having her business featured on my blog. As we started emailing back and forth, it became obvious there was potential for collaboration beyond Young Adult Money. I now have the opportunity to publish and sell my spreadsheets on her site and receive a share of the revenue they bring in. Hello passive side hustle income!

FREE TRIP TO HAWAII

Earlier, I mentioned that entering giveaways was a side hustle of mine. What I didn't mention was the biggest prize I ever won: a trip to Hawaii.

I won the trip through a referral competition that the company IZEA put on. IZEA had a new platform for brokering social media advertisements and wanted more people to sign up for it. I ended up referring the most people during the two-week period the contest ran for and won the Hawaii trip.

If I hadn't started a blog, I would never have built the audience or network necessary to get the referrals needed to win the competition.

THIS BOOK

If it wasn't for my blog, I would never have had the opportunity to write this book, or at least would not have had the opportunity to partner with an incredible publisher like Mango. My advice to people who have a goal of publishing a book is the same as my advice for those looking to break into freelance writing: start a blog.

While I primarily focused on my blogging side hustle in this section, it's important for me to point out that this isn't the only side hustle that has had networking benefits.

One of my other side hustles, spreadsheet consulting, led to an offer to be a Finance Director for a business I had consulted with. While I ultimately did not take the job, it goes to show that having a side hustle can very quickly lead to job offers and new career opportunities.

What side hustles can offer you is this: the ability to simultaneously pay down your debt with your 9-5 income while also building your business. I have many friends who have started photography, freelance writing, or some other type of side hustle that eventually turned into a full-time job. Starting a business as a side hustle allows you to build up clientele through a network of clients, as well as establish clients who will consistently refer you.

NEW SKILLS THAT HELP WITH YOUR 9-5

Having a side hustle can help you attain new or improved skills for your 9-5. That's one reason why I think it's ideal to find a side hustle that blends something you enjoy doing with something that requires skills that are transferable to your full-time job.

It was early on in my post-college career that I took up spreadsheet consulting as a side hustle. Since I was an accountant at the time, you can imagine that what I learned during my side hustle directly benefitted me in my 9-5. It also forced me to explore options and formulas in a spreadsheet that I otherwise would not have looked into.

Some skills you gain during a side hustle aren't as transferable, or at least the value of the skill you developed doesn't seem to mesh with your 9-5. That seemed to be the case with blogging, but through blogging I've gained better people skills and negotiating skills, as I oftentimes have to discuss and negotiate with brand managers and business owners in the day-to-day management of my blog.

One strategic way to think about your side hustle is by focusing on a skill you need to improve for your 9-5. If you're not much of a people person or you do not enjoy public speaking, you could develop those skills by taking on a side hustle that forces you to work directly with people. It may not be comfortable at first, but the nice thing about a side hustle is that you have nothing to lose; you can always quit and start a new one.

Getting paid to develop skills that will help with your 9-5 is a great way to approach your side hustle. It could result in making more money at your 9-5 and you can't beat getting paid to develop your skills.

FINANCIAL CONFIDENCE

As someone who has spent a lot of time thinking, reading, and writing about personal finances, I think one thing is undeniable: debt leads to fear. Those who are comfortable financially have that base level of fear removed and have "better" things to worry about, such as accomplishing goals in their career or business, being in optimal health, creating a schedule that allows for maximum time doing things they love, and so on. If you are struggling with debt, it's impossible to focus as much as you'd like on those "next level" concerns.

Don't get me wrong, some people who seem to be well off have even more debt and fear of finances than others, but I'm focused on the fear that comes from living paycheck-to-paycheck, having a boatload of debt, or simply not feeling confident about your financial situation.

I've been there. I have lots of goals in life but can't even begin to focus on those bigger goals when I have a large amount of student loan debt hanging over my head. Sometimes a 9-5 income just won't cut it. Even a "good" salary typically doesn't allow for quickly and drastically paying down student loans.

This is where a side hustle provides you the one thing that can potentially transform your life: financial confidence.

It's incredible the psychological effect making even a little money outside of your 9-5 can have on your life. Even making $500 or $1,000 extra a month can provide a financial confidence that was impossible with just your 9-5 income. Part of that comes from the fact that side hustle income is something that you need to proactively pursue; no one forces you to pursue a side hustle.

Bringing in a little bit of money outside of your 9-5 forces you to realize that it's entirely possible to increase your income if you are motivated enough. You aren't bound by your 9-5 income.

This isn't to say that a 9-5 is a bad thing. There are many people who work side hustles who have no intention of quitting their 9-5. Some of those people even make more money through their side hustle than their full-time job.

Even if you pay off all your debt, there is still a huge upside to having a side hustle. We'll discuss that next.

AFTER DEBT: HOW SIDE HUSTLES CAN LAUNCH YOU AHEAD FINANCIALLY

It may be difficult to imagine having no debt, but if you are motivated and curious enough to be reading this book I'm confident that you will eventually pay off all your debt. It may not be for one year, five years, or ten years, but you'll get there.

If you pay off your debt using side hustles, you have a huge advantage over other people. Because you've been utilizing a second income stream to pay off your debt, once that debt is gone, the secondary income stream no longer goes towards debt and instead starts to build in your bank account. This makes it much easier to get ahead because you have an entire "bonus" income stream to utilize.

While you may not be as motivated to side hustle with debt no longer hanging over your head, getting ahead financially can serve as a new motivation. Think of the impact that even an extra $1,000 a month can have on your finances.

If you make $1,000 in side hustle income every month for the next 10 years and deposit it into an investment account that makes 8% interest, with interest compounded monthly, you will have approximately $184,000 at the end of the 10 years.[9]

That's enough to buy a rental property for cash that can be used as a passive income source for the rest of your life. Or if you bought a stock like AT&T with approximately a 5.5% dividend yield, you would have passive income of around $10,000 a year. If you made $2,000 a month in side hustle income during those 10 years, you'd have a whopping $368,000 to invest, which results in a little over $20,000 a year in passive income (if you invest in a stock with a dividend yield of 5.5%).

Remember this is all in addition to your full-time income, which is why side hustle income is such a great way to get ahead financially.

9. http://www.thecalculatorsite.com/finance/calculators/
compoundinterestcalculator.php

131

ADVANCED SIDE HUSTLE POTENTIAL

One way that side hustles provide upside is through what I like to call advanced side hustle potential. Earlier I mentioned the idea of a side hustle that involves creating, manufacturing, and selling a unique product. This side hustle will typically require thousands of dollars of money up-front and simply isn't feasible for most people who are working to pay off debt and build a solid financial base.

Think of this scenario. You have been working your side hustle for a couple years now. You have leveraged your side hustle income to offset your debt payments, save an emergency fund, and have some money left over. The "extra" money could be used to invest in another side hustle, such as the unique product side hustle, that you otherwise would not be able to take on.

Leveraging side hustle income to take on a second side hustle is a great way to invest in something that you wouldn't use your regular 9-5 income for. It also allows you to take on risk that you otherwise wouldn't be comfortable taking on.

Another example of an advanced side hustle technique is utilizing your first side hustle to scale your business. Some successful bloggers scale their side hustle by starting or purchasing additional blogs. This allows for utilizing the same resource pool across multiple blogs. For example, instead of hiring a writer for your site, you can hire a writer to write across three different websites.

Side hustles may seem like a grind, especially if you choose one that doesn't pay anything at first. Even when you are making money, it can be exhausting spending your spare time working.

Focusing on the potential upside, as well as the inevitable financial benefits of side hustles, can help you stay motivated even when you don't want to hustle. Keep your eyes open for opportunities to leverage your side hustle and always remember why you started side hustling in the first place.

in thousands $

Year	Year Deposits	Year Interest	Total Deposits	Total Interest	Balance
1	$0	$1	$12	$1	$13
2	$12	$2	$24	$2	$26
3	$12	$3	$36	$5	$41
4	$12	$4	$48	$9	$77
5	$12	$5	$60	$14	$74
6	$12	$7	$72	$21	$93
7	$12	$8	$84	$29	$113
8	$12	$10	$96	$39	$135
9	$12	$12	$108	$50	$158
10	$12	$14	$120	$64	$184

Side Hustle Hacks

Hacks

Chapter 10

S ide hustles can be exciting in the short-term but can quickly start feeling like a burden, making them difficult to maintain. It's easy to side hustle when your motivation is high, but what about a year in when you just want a break? Or what if you get sick of the work as you write your 500th blog post, or respond to your 3,000th email? When will it stop?

Side hustling can be difficult to integrate into your life, but for many people the benefits of side hustles outweigh the negatives, so they stick with it. If you are proactive enough to start a side hustle in the first place, you clearly have the initiative to solve problems by taking action versus sitting back and dwelling on your misfortune.

This chapter is about how to side hustle better. After all, if you can side hustle better, why wouldn't you? It can be the difference between working on your side hustle 20 hours a week versus working on it 10 hours a week, or the difference between being able to juggle everything versus hitting a wall and burning out.

Let's kick it off by talking about the skills to focus on if you want to be successful at side hustles.

SKILLS TO FOCUS ON FOR A SUCCESSFUL SIDE HUSTLE

Besides being motivated by a financial goal, I think there are a few specific skills that help people succeed when they side hustle. Here are 5 skills that I recommend people focus on improving if they want to successfully integrate side hustling into their life:

TIME MANAGEMENT

Earlier in the book I talked about evaluating whether or not you have the capacity for a side hustle. It's not easy to fit a side hustle into an already-packed schedule, but it is possible. It probably isn't surprising that those who are able to successfully side hustle are great at time management.

Starting and sticking with a side hustle will be very difficult if you aren't in the pattern of planning your time. Getting better at time management can be as simple as sticking to a calendar and saying "no" to things.

If you don't currently use a calendar app like Outlook or Google Calendar, you will want to get started ASAP. Yes, that includes planning out your evenings and weekends. You need to set aside blocks of time for your side hustle, and for everything else, if you want to be successful. One reason why side hustles like waiting tables or delivering food are sometimes easier than more flexible side hustles is because you are forced to stick to a schedule.

ABILITY TO PRIORITIZE

Being able to prioritize is another essential skill for any successful side hustler. Having a side hustle means you have limited free time, because some (or most) is being eaten up by your side hustle. So in your limited free time, are you able to pick and choose what's important enough for your time and attention? Said differently, are you able to let the unimportant things slide?

It's easy to try and "do it all," but it's not sustainable. On a typical weekend, you aren't going to be able to work out three times, clean your whole house, deal with all of life's responsibilities, get 8 hours of sleep a night, spend a bunch of time with friends and family, and work 12 hours on your side hustle. Something's gotta give! This is where picking and choosing priorities matter. If your side hustle isn't a priority, you aren't going to stick with it long-term.

If you have a side hustle where you can work on any given task on a long to-do list, it becomes even more important to decide what matters and what doesn't. Anyone who has started a blog knows you could spend 24/7 doing things to improve your site, but the reality is that 20% of the work is going to give 80% of the results. Being able to recognize this and follow through with only focusing on what matters is something that everyone can get better at.

ABILITY TO ADAPT TO CHANGING SITUATIONS

One day I got an email around 9AM from an advertiser saying they would compensate me $150 if I published a review of a 45 minute documentary. There was a catch: the review had to be up by 2PM. And this was on a weekday.

Instead of letting the opportunity pass, I reached out to a friend who had made the transition to a full-time freelance writer. She was able to write the review and get it published before the deadline, and everyone involved benefited.

Being able to adapt to changing situations is a critical skill for people who side hustle. It's a bit ironic that this skill is in the same list as "time management," but they really can work together. If a time-sensitive opportunity comes your way, are you able to manage your time to make it work? Or will you miss out because you can't adapt?

FOCUS ON THE BOTTOM LINE

You don't have to be an accountant to know that focusing on the bottom line is important in any job or business. The bottom line is the amount of money that will eventually go into your bank account, so it needs to be a huge focus of your side hustle.

How can you get better at "focusing on the bottom line?" By consistently evaluating whether what you are doing is the best use of your time for the amount of money you are getting paid. For some people, taking on a part-time job as a side hustle makes good financial sense because they need money ASAP. For others, it might make sense to seek out a side hustle that has potential for higher $/hour, but is not necessarily consistent, at least not in the beginning.

This ties into being able to prioritize effectively. While it can be ambiguous with some side hustles, it's important to at least ask yourself "how is this impacting my bottom line?" You may find that some of the things you have on your to-do list really aren't going to impact your bottom line and are more likely just "nice to have." Time is too precious with a side hustle: drop those unprofitable tasks!

TECHNICAL SKILLS

Having technical skills isn't always essential for doing well in a side hustle, but for certain side hustles it can be a huge help. If you are starting a side hustle that requires you to learn and utilize various software programs, it's essential that you have at least basic technical skills. If it takes you days or weeks to learn a software program that is essential to your business, you are going to struggle simply because side hustles force you to operate on a shorter timeline.

If you aren't tech-savvy or do not enjoy working on computers, don't pursue a side hustle that is dependent on your technical skills. You will likely burn out from the hours of training that will be required to keep up. You'll be better off pursuing something that plays more to your strengths.

These are a few of the skills that I think people should focus on if they want to succeed in side hustles. Remember, time is precious when it comes to side hustles. You are automatically limited by the fact that you are trying to pursue something on top of a full-time job.

ONLINE TOOLS THAT HELP WITH SIDE HUSTLES

There are literally hundreds of apps that can help you run a side hustle better. I'll share a few that I have found to be useful. These will be more applicable to people running an online side hustle but there are some apps that are relevant to virtually any side hustle.

GOOGLE CALENDAR

It's much easier to stick to a calendar when you are able to update it from your phone. Google Calendar is the ideal calendar app because you can update it on the go and it syncs between your computer and phone. I use my Google Calendar religiously.

GOOGLE DRIVE

I think of Google Drive as serving a similar function as Microsoft Office, but cloud-based. There is a word processing application (Google Docs), a spreadsheet application (Google Sheets), and a PowerPoint-like application (Google Slides).

The biggest benefit of Google Drive is that multiple people can be in a file at the same time and everyone can edit simultaneously. Also, editing and sharing is as simple as going to the URL associated with the document or spreadsheet.

I have an editorial calendar for my blog where my writers can see what topic I have scheduled for them on which day, as well as make edits to the calendar themselves. I've used Google Docs in the past to post job openings.

DROPBOX

Dropbox is a cloud storage application that is free to use up to a certain amount of storage space. This has been a lifesaver when I have a large file to share with someone and I'm unable to send it to them via email. In fact, I would argue that it's even easier and more practical to share files via Dropbox than over email.

MICROSOFT OUTLOOK

Yes, we all know email is useful, so why am I calling out Microsoft Outlook? Microsoft Outlook is easier to use than web-based apps like Gmail and has more options and functionality. It was a few years ago that I first synced my Gmail and website email to Outlook and it's been a lifesaver from a productivity and efficiency standpoint.

BUFFER

If you are active on social media, Buffer is an essential app. With Buffer you can schedule social media posts on Twitter and Facebook. You can schedule for specific times or you can choose to put posts in your queue that will be posted at set times each day. Pricing starts at $10/month or $102/year.

TAILWIND

Tailwind is similar to Buffer but is made for Pinterest. You can schedule pins and view analytics that tell you the most effective time to pin. It costs $10/month to use Tailwind.

GUMROAD

Gumroad is a website that makes it easy to sell virtual products online. Many people sell courses, ebooks, music, and more through the Gumroad website. There is a transaction fee of

$0.25 for each sale as well as a 5% charge per sold product. There are no monthly fees. Gumroad allows sellers to focus on their products instead of managing a sale and delivery system, and makes it easy to accept virtually any type of payment.

PAYPAL

As an online side-hustler, I swear by PayPal. I've used it on a weekly basis for more than three years now and it's the absolute easiest way to send and receive payments. While there are transaction fees, it typically has been worth it considering how easy and universal PayPal is.

These are just a few examples of applications that will make your life easier as a side hustler. There are tons of other apps that you may find useful as you try to organize and streamline your side hustle, but these are the ones that I would highly recommend checking out.

TIME HACKS FOR SIDE HUSTLES

Not to beat a dead horse, but time is important with side hustles. Finding ways to create more time for yourself is extremely important.

Regardless of what side hustle you have, there are a few things you can do to free up time.

AVOID RUSH HOUR

Do you have an hour-plus commute to work due to rush hour? If you can't shift your work hours around, consider going to the library or a coffee shop after work and working on your to-do list for an hour or two. Not only will you get a lot done but you'll also cut your commute time down by 1/2 or even 1/3 of what it would be.

HIRE HELP AROUND YOUR HOME

Want to have some free time, but also want to side hustle? You may need to outsource some work around your home. This could mean having someone come clean once a week or paying someone to mow your lawn. It could also mean hiring out work instead of going the do-it-yourself route. Remember, though, that to justify outsourcing you need to make more per hour than you are paying the person you are outsourcing to.

FIND UNEXPECTED TIMES TO WORK

Early mornings. A 5-minute break. Lunch time. 30 minutes before going to bed. While you are on a treadmill. Find those obscure times where you are able to quickly crank out some work and you will be surprised just how much you can get done during time that otherwise would have been spent doing unproductive things.

FOCUS AND CONCENTRATION

Online side hustles are the worst when it comes to distractions and it can be difficult to focus on the task at hand. If you're at home working on your computer, there will always be a hundred distractions. If you focus during work time, you could end up cutting the amount of time you spend on your side hustle while getting the same results from a productivity and financial aspect. Limit distractions whenever possible.

Using these hacks to better utilize your time will result in less stress and more free time. Stop browsing Facebook and Twitter when you should be working on things that actually provide value!

SIDE HUSTLES AND TAXES: HOW TO PREPARE FOR TAX TIME

Preparing for taxes starts well before tax time, especially if you have a side hustle. Side hustles are not like 9-5 jobs. No one is taking out taxes each paycheck. Heck, with many side hustles, regular paychecks simply are not part of the deal.

Even if your side hustle is working a part-time job it's virtually a guarantee your employer is not taking out enough taxes. From a payroll perspective, they view the money they pay you as the only money you make, meaning they are likely taking out little to no money for your taxes. It's up to you to voluntarily have your 9-5 employer take out additional money from your taxes or to set aside money in a savings account in case you get hit with a big tax bill.

If you have side hustle income from contract work or a business and expect to make over $1,000 in income in a given tax year, you are required to pay quarterly estimated taxes. Quarterly estimated taxes require some guesswork, as side hustle income can fluctuate and your other finances also impact how much you owe (i.e. deductions, income from your 9-5, etc.).[10]

To get the full tax value out of your side hustle, it's important to keep excellent records of your income and expenses. Whether you keep copies of checks and receipts in a folder or keep everything in an Excel Spreadsheet, you need to find a system that works for you.

One thing I would highly recommend is opening a separate checking account for your side hustle. This helps keep your personal and business finances separate and will make tracking just a little bit easier.

For my side hustle, I use both Google Docs and Excel to track and reconcile my finances. I also utilize PayPal and a small business checking account, and avoid having any of my business transactions hit my personal checking account. If I want to take a "dividend" from my side hustle, I shift money from my business checking to my personal. It makes it much easier to go back and reconcile my finances come tax time.

10. For a more thorough review of quarterly estimated taxes, including tips on how to calculate them and when they are due, check out this resource page on Young Adult Money http://www.YoungAdultMoney.com/QuarterlyTaxesHowTo/

Pulling it All Together

Chapter 11

S o far we've gone over what to do before starting a side hustle, how to find the right side hustle for you, ideas for starting side hustles, and side hustle "hacks" that give your side hustle a better chance of succeeding.

In this chapter, I want to briefly focus on two important topics: sticking with a side hustle and deciding when to quit.

While starting a side hustle is a great first step, the reality is that over time the attractiveness of a side hustle might wear off. You might get burnt out from your side hustle, lose interest, or start questioning whether you should continue your side hustle. Another dilemma that happens to many people who side hustle is deciding when to abandon their current side hustle for another opportunity.

STICKING WITH A SIDE HUSTLE

In the blogging world, there is a general consensus that a large majority of bloggers quit within the first six months. I'm not sure anyone has ever actually proven this, but it does seem to be fairly accurate.

There are a few reasons this happens. Initially, blogging is a fun and glamorous thing to pursue. It's likely the first time the person has ever started a blog. There are fun new features and, unbelievably, there are a handful of people actually visiting the blog!

Over time, though, it becomes a grind. Constantly thinking up new topics, networking with other bloggers, managing social media, dealing with technical issues, and other work that comes with owning a blog becomes frustrating and not fun like it was in the beginning. Plus, blog traffic is likely going up slowly and there is a virtual guarantee that the blog is making pennies a day, if that.

So bloggers quit.

What can bloggers do differently to give themselves a better chance of getting past the six month mark? It's all about preparation.

HAVING A PLAN OF ACTION BEFORE STARTING

This may sound repetitive, but it cannot be understated: have a plan before starting a side hustle. If you don't have a plan, your chances of sticking with a side hustle long-term are low.

Some things to think about when making your plan are:

How long do I plan on doing this side hustle?

- Six months? Indefinitely?
- Will I drop this side hustle if a more attractive opportunity comes along?

What is my ultimate goal with this side hustle?

- Create a new income stream to offset debt payments?
- Save x dollars for a specific goal (i.e. trip abroad)?
- Potentially start a new career?
- Make enough money to quit my job?

How much time per week will this side hustle take?

- Do I have capacity for this side hustle?
- How will I react if this side hustle takes more hours per week than I originally thought?

How will I free up time for this side hustle? How will I set up my schedule to accommodate this side hustle?

How long am I committing to this side hustle before I will allow myself to consider quitting?

- If I don't make money by _____ I will consider quitting
- I will stick with this side hustle for _____ months before considering quitting

Why are you really looking for a side hustle?

How will this side hustle benefit me in other areas of my life?

Is this side hustle playing to my strengths?

Will I enjoy this side hustle? Is there a side hustle I might enjoy more?

Does this side hustle conflict with my 9-5?

- Will it ever conflict from a timing perspective?
- Is there any potential conflict of interest with this side hustle?

What opportunities do I hope will come out of this side hustle? What can I do to make those opportunities more likely?

Thinking through why you are starting a side hustle, how you will make it work, and what your ultimate goal is, are all important things to recognize and reflect on before starting a side hustle. Remember, the goal here is to give your side hustle the best chance of succeeding. If you don't know what your goals are for your side hustle, it will be difficult to recognize whether you are successful or not, and especially difficult recognizing reasons why you were or were not successful.

I used to read a blog called Deliver Away Debt where the blogger's goal with his side hustle was to deliver pizzas on top of his full-time job to aggressively pay down debt. From what I read, it seemed like a difficult endeavor, as he was taking time away from his family and sacrificing sleep to make his side hustle a success. He ultimately was successful in paying off his debt through the increased income and I can't help but think he was able to persevere because he knew exactly what he was trying to accomplish with his side hustle.

KNOW WHEN TO QUIT

You can spend years planning for something and still have it not work out the way you envisioned it. The problem with planning is that it's based on assumptions, and some of those assumptions are bound to change.

Perhaps you assumed that you would be at the same job the next three years, but you end up getting a new job that requires 10-20 more hours of your time each week...and those were the 10-20 hours a week you had planned on contributing to your side hustle.

Now what do you do? Do you quit? Do you adjust your side hustle?

Sometimes the answer is obvious. If you previously worked 7-4 and then worked a part-time job 6-9, but are now stuck in the office as late as 6pm at times, your part-time job side hustle likely won't be sustainable.

Other times, the answer is less obvious. When I shifted from corporate accounting to corporate finance, I wanted to contribute more time and energy towards my full-time job. Instead of abandoning my blog (which I think is a terrible idea for an established blog, especially a profitable one) I outsourced more of the writing. I still brokered all the advertising deals, edited the posts, and managed social media, but taking writing out of the equation freed up some time and energy to put towards other pursuits.

Two things I think you need to consider before quitting a side hustle are: what is being given up in return for quitting? and, are there options for changing your side hustle in a way that allows you to continue?

WHAT IS BEING SACRIFICED WHEN YOU QUIT A SIDE HUSTLE?

There was a point in time where I considered selling my blog. At the time I wasn't having as much fun running it as I used to, and was a bit burnt out from blogging. I also wanted to pursue some other opportunities in my spare time.

Selling my blog would have required a lot of work in itself. I would have had to create detailed documentation of all user accounts, financials, advertiser relationships, and more. Having been in the blogosphere for quite some time, I knew that there were a number of improvements that I could implement that would have almost immediately made the site more valuable.

So I didn't sell and continued to operate it as I had been for the previous three years.

I'm glad I did. Since tabling the idea of selling my blog, I've landed two large advertising deals with major brands. I also was given the opportunity to write this book which would not have been possible if I had sold my site. By not selling, I continued to expose myself to the upside of major advertising deals, a book deal, and more.

The point I'm trying to illustrate is that you have to really think hard about what you are giving up when you quit a side hustle. The income you receive from your side hustle is typically not all you are giving up. You are also giving up the potential upside that comes with your side hustle. Of course, that also means you are not gaining precious "free time" that is likely motivating you to consider quitting in the first place.

HOW CAN YOU CHANGE/ ALTER YOUR SIDE HUSTLE?

If you're considering quitting your side hustle, it's important to first evaluate how you can change your side hustle to be more accommodating to your schedule and lifestyle.

Some side hustles are easier to quit or take time off from than others. If you are working a part-time job at a gym on the weekend, it could be relatively easy to take a few months off and then start again. With some small business and online side hustles, momentum can make it difficult to slow down because if you stop or quit it may cause you to miss out on some big opportunities that were just around the corner.

Before quitting a side hustle, I highly encourage you to not only think about what you are sacrificing by quitting, but how you can make your side hustle work within your schedule. Can you outsource any of the work? Can you cut back on the income you take home from your side hustle in return for having someone else take on some of the work? Can you cut back your hours and time dedicated to your side hustle? Will you be able to pick it up again down the road? Do you care whether you are never involved in this side hustle again? All good questions to ask yourself before quitting.

Quitting a side hustle isn't a bad thing. Many successful side hustlers and entrepreneurs have quit their side hustle or drastically changed their approach. Sometimes sticking with a side hustle prevents you from taking advantage of more lucrative or fulfilling opportunities. Weigh the pros and cons and trust your instincts.

FINAL NOTE

Regardless of whether you are struggling with debt from college, credit cards, or something else, there is a proactive solution you can take to get rid of your debt: side hustles. You can conquer your debt and improve your finances through side hustles.

There are countless people today that are using side hustles to do just that. There's the parents who have started a small business to fund their children's education. There's the new grad who is managing social media accounts of local businesses to offset their student loans. There's the twenty-something that runs a tutoring business on the weekend to pay off their credit card debt.

The options are endless. What will you do?

It's time to hustle away debt.

AFTERWORD

Hustle Away Debt embodies a certain attitude and approach to debt that I think more people need to consider: taking your income into your own hands through side hustles.

This book did not happen overnight and the concept behind it has been something that I've been thinking about – and practicing – for years now. My hope is that this book will help thousands of people struggling with debt – student loan or otherwise – increase their income and start living the lifestyle they desire.

Furthermore, I hope that through this book people realize it is possible to integrate side hustles into their lives and that they can have a big impact.

This book wouldn't have been possible without the help and support of many people.

Thanks to my wife for putting up with the craziness of having a side hustler for a husband who works a full-time job, runs a blog in his "free" time, and somehow still found time to write this book.

To my editor, Hugo Villabona, who kept me on track throughout the process, Erika Shoemaker, for initially reaching out to me about writing this book, and everyone else at Mango Media who had a hand in making this book a reality.

To Stefanie O'Connell for writing a wonderful foreword for the book.

To Marla Urban for reading a draft of the book cover-to-cover and providing excellent feedback and edits.

To all my blogging colleagues and friends who provided input and encouragement throughout the process.

And finally to all my readers – old and new – for their support.